SURVIVOR ONCE SURVIVOR FOR LIFE

SURVIVOR ONCE SURVIVOR FOR LIFE

OVERCOMER OF CANCER, DEATH OF A MARRIAGE,
AND DEATH OF A PARENT

SARAH S. JOHNSON

Copyright© 2020 Sarah S. Johnson

All rights reserved worldwide. No part of this book may be reproduced or transmitted in any form or by any means electronic or mechanical, including photocopying, recording or by any information storage and retrieval system without written permission from Sarah S. Johnson.

Website: Survivoroncesurvivorforlife.com
Email: Sapphirajenterprise@gmail.com

Editor: Emerge Editing & Writing -Daphney M. Chaney
Photographer: Omar Ramos Photography

All Scripture quotations, unless otherwise indicated, are taken from the Holy Bible, Life Application Study Bible®, King James®. Copyright © 2004 by Tyndale House Publishers, Inc. Used by permission of Tyndale House Publishers, Inc., Carol Stream, Illinois 60188. All rights reserved. Scripture quotations are taken from the Holy Bible, New International Version® Copyright © 2011 by Holy Bible Zondervan. Used by permission of Zondervan, Grand Rapid, Michigan. All rights reserved. Scripture quotations are taken from the Amplified Bible (AMP). 1954, 1958, 1962, 1965, 1987 by The Lockman Foundation. Used by Permission.

ISBN: 978-0-9988646-0-0

1. Autobiography 2. Inspirational 3. Christian

Printed in the United States of America

Disclaimer/Warning: This book is intended for lecture and informative purposes only. This publication is designed to provide competent and reliable information regarding the subject matter covered. Neither the author or publisher are engaged in rendering legal or professional advice. Laws vary from state to state and if legal, financial, or other expert assistance is needed, the services of a professional should be sought. The author and publisher disclaim any liability that is incurred from the use or application of the contents of this book.

DEDICATION

This book is dedicated to my children, Cornelius, Faith, Kennedy, Dinasti and Destini.
Thank you for allowing me to write my first book.
I appreciate your willingness to help so I could complete this project.
Thank you for sharing me, as I encourage others to believe that they too are survivors.
Thank you for loving me unconditionally.
I count it an honor and privilege that God chose me to be your mother.
Mommy loves you, Neilus, Faifai, Kenken, Sissy and Desi!

ACKNOWLEDGMENTS

I would like to thank the Most-High God for the blueprint for this book, the gift of writing and the ability to hear the things that were downloaded into my spirit.

I would like to thank my mother, Deborah Simmons, for making me a "kept baby."

I know that my father, the late Robert Lee Hooper, would be proud of this major accomplishment.

I would like to send a special "thank you" to the troubles I have seen. Trouble, I know your intent was to destroy me. Instead, you ushered me into the arms of my Heavenly Father. Trouble, I salute you. After all, if it was not for you, there would be no book to help others.

TABLE OF CONTENTS

Foreword	xi
Introduction	1
Chapter 1: The Path	5
Chapter 2: Permission Granted	11
Chapter 3: You Name It	19
Chapter 4: It's Not Your Choice	31
Chapter 5: Groomed To Do It	35
Chapter 6: Divine Timing	43
Chapter 7: Yours, Not Theirs	53
Chapter 8: Let the Walls Fall Down	61
Chapter 9: You Vs. Them	69
Chapter 10: Your Life, Your Dreams, Your Way	81
Chapter 11: Survivor of the Threshold	91
Chapter 12: Running Out of Gas	99
Chapter 13: Free Yourself, Forgive Yourself	107
Chapter 14: The Benefits of Rejection & Abandonment	119
Conclusion: Survivor Once Survivor For Life	135

FOREWORD

Sometimes in life, we don't get what we deserve, but we get what we need to shape our lives. For believers in Jesus Christ, getting us to our purpose is the only thing that matters to God.

With the manifestation of His purpose comes plenty of pain along with an unending process that's designed to build us and not break us.

From the beginning of time, there has always been challenges to overcome, especially in coming into wholeness, harmony and alignment to God's will. Seemingly, God takes us down a long road that's full of bumps, curves and sharp turns before things smooth out. I personally know the pain that ultimately reveals purpose. So much so, that I have given my entire life to help others realize and fulfill God's plan.

Sarah Johnson has given us a front row seat into her broken but brave journey and how she took the missing pieces of her life and allowed God to strategically intertwine them and use them for His glory. She displays both courage and determination.

I believe that although Sarah has survived a lot of things, it's very clear to me and it will be to you too as you read her story, that she is so much more than just a survivor, she is more than a conqueror through Christ that has loved her (Romans 8:37b).

*Survivor Once, Survivor for Lif*e is not just a book, but it is a tool that will boost your faith, reignite your passion, challenge your mind and even tug on your heart strings to show you how to truly live a victorious life.

Prophetess Barbara Calloway
Barbara Calloway Ministries
www.BarbaraCallowayMinistries.org

INTRODUCTION

You are stronger than you think! A lot of what you have endured has overtaken others… overtaken them in their minds and their ability to get up and fight. I challenge you to change your perspective on how you see "trying" situations. I knew I was a natural born fighter. I had no idea of the extent and degree to what my Heavenly Father placed on the inside of me. During the birthing of this book, I was diagnosed with vocal cord cancer, received divorce papers three days before starting radiation treatment, and supported my father until he passed away. I lived through all of this within five months in 2014.

According to the enemy of my soul, 2014 was designed to take me out of here. Actually, I should be sitting in a corner somewhere rocking and losing my mind. But, I thank God for His plans for my life. It was necessary for me to go through what was meant to kill me! God needed a model to demonstrate His work, His strength and His grace.

I did not understand, but I told God throughout the process, my answer was still "yes." God's grace fortified me through every season of opposition. I quickly learned the cost of yes. God purges us by shedding dead things. Many people want God to use them, but foolishly think that they can pick and choose what battles they will face.

The purpose of this book is to provide encouragement to those that have faced or are currently facing difficult situations. I challenge each reader to consider shifting their perspective while finding the good in everything they face. As atrocious as cancer is, it has given me a new lease on life. It led me to make many decisions that I would have never considered. I've also enjoyed doing things alone, such as traveling. One of the greatest lessons I've learned is letting go of bitterness and forgiving those who have hurt me.

Because of the hurt, abandonment, and rejection I faced, I felt that I was a great candidate to receive inner and emotional healing. From the cancer diagnosis, I was able to address the hurt that I was currently experiencing by uncovering the deep layers of pain that stemmed from by childhood.

In fact, it was the reminders of all the difficulties that I experienced in my past that helped me to keep going. Each difficult experience served as a reference point for me that if He brought me through before, then He would bring me through this time.

It was during this time that I was able to pour from my heart. Although I received several prophetic words regarding book authorship, I did not know where or how to start. I attended a conference in Arlington, Texas, where I received a prophetic word from God. A prophet asked me if I had started writing my book. At that time, writing a book was the furthest thing from my mind.

I went home that night and prayed and asked God, "If what the man of God said is really from You, then give me the blueprint for this book."

I didn't want just any words on paper. I wanted the words to be inspired by God. I envisioned each reader identifying with my journey and knowing the redeeming and resurrecting power of God. I want each reader to know that the same God that saw me through my darkest times is the same God that will see them through their difficult situations. That same night, I wrote the first chapter of the book.

God allowed you to survive so that He can use you as part of His rescue team. You had to go through it. At the appointed time, you will share it because you are a SURVIVOR!

CHAPTER 1

THE PATH

Have you ever wondered why God chose the parents He chose for us? I often look around and ask God, "Why was I born into my family?"

It appears the people who lack motivation to do anything in life have the world's greatest support systems, while those of us who are driven, lack that very thing. Don't get me wrong, I am thankful for the life I have. I personally would have preferred more support and love, but I am sure there is a reason that everything I've accomplished has been met with an insurmountable level of hardship and difficulty. In fact, for a very long time, I did not like my life nor my family.

I never understood why God chose my mother and father to be my parents. I've always felt cheated because both of my parents were deaf. I felt cheated because I had to be the ears for my mom. Before I could enjoy being a child, I had adult responsibilities. I often missed school because my mother needed my assistance. A lot of times, I had to accompany her everywhere she went so that I could speak for her.

None of the other adults in my family felt like it was too much for me as a child to assume adult like responsibilities, therefore, no one spoke up for me. As a result, they essentially robbed me of my childhood. The benefit of having the support of a village significantly reduces the burdens being placed upon the shoulders of one person. I do believe there was a better solution that could have involved the entire family, but no one considered it. I was provided a roof over my head and food to eat; however, my emotional needs were not met.

I am not angry at my mom for the decisions that she made. However, I wish she had some guidance and wisdom regarding age appropriate responsibilities for a child. The other adults in my family seemed too preoccupied with their own lives and because they were not directly impacted, it appeared that they ignored the great burden that was placed upon me. Silently, I wished someone would have rescued me, but no one did. And the person I felt should have protected and nurtured me was the first person to exploit me. I find that this issue is far too common in families, especially within the black community. There were many adults who could have called the rest of the family together to come up with a viable solution to aid my mother in her disability. I'm not bitter and do have sympathy for my mom. Please understand that you can be compassionate and still strongly disagree with the way a person handles things. I cannot reiterate enough that there was a better way for her to receive the support that she needed.

Little did I know that my Heavenly Father was using what I lacked in my childhood and the early responsibilities to work for my good. The enemy of our soul does not fight fair. He began his ambush against me when I was just a child, most vulnerable, and unable to think or reason for myself. The enemy's intentions were for me to be a statistic, but God intervened on my behalf. Being born to deaf parents, along with being robbed of my childhood, was the beginning of my becoming a yielded vessel to God.

My life was the epitome of low socioeconomic status. I knew we were poor. My mother, sister, and I lived in one room during my childhood and teenage years, so there was no such thing as privacy. We saw very little of our father, although he'd visit us maybe three times a year. His concerns seemed genuine, and he'd ask for our clothing and shoe sizes, but never delivered on his promises. And because my father showed partiality toward my siblings, he was instrumental in introducing pain and rejection into my life. His inability to parent me, as I needed him to, was the catalyst of emotional heartbreak and disappointment.

As you can see, the people who were chosen to parent me, were also the people who introduced pain, rejection, and abandonment into my life. Please allow me to interject right here…this is not an attempt to "throw my parents under the bus" because I know they truly care about me.

After reading the first part of my journey, I'm sure that you can understand why I questioned God regarding my family. I am also sure that you can see the pain that I felt was valid. While I am positive both of my parents did the best that they could; I now know that my parents could not nurture and love me beyond the love and nurture they received themselves. Eventually, I matured and was able to love them where they were. When I became a parent myself, I made the mistake in measuring my parents according to my standards. Honestly, my standards were shaped around my perceptions. Our perceptions can only go as far as our experiences or reference points from others.

My parents could not go beyond their level of maturity in parenting. It can be compared to two people who are required to take a standardized test to measure their analytical abilities. Imagine there are two people who never graduated high school and were expected to do well on a test without any previous skill or training. And their employer attempting to base their continued employment on how well they performed on the standardized test. Sounds insane, right? Well, just like the Human Resource Department for a company who would adhere to the employer's disclosure agreement, where no employee could be terminated based on the lack of skill the employer was made aware of (via resume and or application), the great news for us is that Jesus is our Human Resources Department Facilitator. He gives us grace for the things we lack. And it is because of that same grace that I've been able to grow beyond resentment and bitterness.

There was something else that taunted me during my childhood and adult life. To add insult to injury, I was molested by a family member during a time other people were at home. The people who should have protected me failed to do so. When I tried to share with my grandmother what happened, I was immediately called out of my name. I was told verbatim, "Bitch, stop lying."

After hearing those words, I was speechless. I did not expect to be told that. I knew better than to challenge my grandmother, so I absorbed her words and held in my pain. I walked away feeling empty. I shared what would be synonymous to the #METOO hashtag and instead of receiving support, I was made to feel worthless. She also projected her viewpoints of me to everyone else, and unfortunately, when she pushed me away, most of my family did also.

I felt as if my voice was silenced, and what I thought or how I felt did not matter because in the eyes of that one person, I was a liar. My attempt to get retribution was far from a lie. In fact, I was called out of my name so much that when others asked my name, I should have repeated what had been spoken to me and over me for years.

As you can see, the enemy of our souls takes the unfortunate events in our lives and causes those things to work against us. This was another situation to further support the negative impact of no one speaking up for me, when I was unable to defend myself.

Emotionally and mentally, I had every reason to cooperate with the enemy. For those who are wondering, how do you cooperate with the enemy? You do so by engaging in destructive behavior. As I began to look back over my life, I could see the patterns of toxic behavior starting to form. However, I could also see the hand of God which reflected as boundaries in my life.

Even though there were times when things appeared to spiral out of control, there was a limit to the foolishness I experienced. At the time, I could not explain how I could engage in an act of destruction, yet not be excited about my behavior. God would always limit the extent of my foolishness.

While in my mess, God remained interested in me. Despite all the hurt, rejection, betrayal, and molestation, God was still with me. God was consistently drawing me by His spirit to come to Him.

> "And I, when I am lifted up from the earth, will draw all people to myself"
> —(John 12:32)

I was the perfect candidate for God to draw by His Spirit. I needed a Savior, and He wanted to show me that He had a plan that was so much bigger than the hurt and pain I was introduced to. God knew me before I entered my mother's womb. The things I had experienced in my childhood were not a surprise to Him.

> "Before I formed you in the womb, I knew you, before you were born, I set you apart; I appointed you as a prophet to the nations"
> —(Jeremiah 1:5)

God, who is the orchestrator of our lives, placed abilities on the inside of us to use as an arsenal against the enemy. The enemy knows that he cannot thwart the plans of God. However, the enemy can try to get us to forfeit the things God desires to do and complete in our lives. When we focus more on the wrong that has been done to us, we put ourselves in position to forfeit those plans.

CHAPTER 2

PERMISSION GRANTED

The affliction I endured set the stage for the hand of God to move mightily in my life. If we allow it, pain can serve as a push to get us to the next level. On the flip side, it can also cause us to become numb to our surroundings. If we focus on every pain we've experienced, it may cause us to miss out on the greater good to come from it.

In 2014, I received a cancer diagnosis. Despite everything I'd previously endured, it appeared to be the worst thing I'd ever faced. I'd also received divorce papers three days before I was to begin radiation treatments. The divorce caused me to feel rejected and abandoned all over again. I'd grown accustomed to not having support, but this time it was different. I did not want to face cancer alone. But I dared not ask for support from him or anyone else, so instead, I embraced my reality.

At first, I thought I would be ok, but when I went to the clinic for treatment and saw the support from the family members and friends of others, my pain grew. I began to wonder what was so horribly wrong with me that I had to face that journey alone? I can count on one hand the people who actually showed up for me. And unfortunately, not everyone who did come to "support" showed up with pure motives. Some of my family wanted to come over just to see if I fit "the look" of a cancer patient. I forced myself to hold back tears, because I understood that my healing was contingent upon my attitude and what I allowed to harbor in my heart. Basically, I had to pretend that things were not as bad as they appeared to be. As a result, I over-compensated in my appearance. As a Mary Kay Independent Beauty Consultant, I intentionally dressed as if I was going to work. That was my way of coping with what I was going through. I could not control the actions and behaviors of others, but I was determined that my appearance would not match the things that were going on in my life. God allowed those trials because of the purpose that would come from those experiences. Pain can cause you to cry out to God, drawing you closer to Him, or pain can cause you to stray away from God in bitterness and anger. During times of hardship, it's easy to think that God has abandoned us; But that isn't true.

Let's look at the story of Hannah:

> *"And her adversary also provoked her sore, for to make her fret, because the Lord had shut up her womb. And as he did so year by year, when she went up to the house of the Lord, so she provoked her; therefore, she wept, and did not eat. Then said Elkanah her husband to her, Hannah, why weepest thou? and why eatest thou not? and why is thy heart grieved? am not I better to thee than ten sons? So Hannah rose up after they had eaten in Shiloh, and after they had drunk. Now Eli the priest sat upon a seat by a post of the temple of the Lord. And she was in*

bitterness of soul, and prayed unto the Lord, and wept sore. And she vowed a vow, and said, O Lord of hosts, if thou wilt indeed look on the affliction of thine handmaid, and remember me, and not forget thine handmaid, but will give unto thine handmaid a man child, then I will give him unto the Lord all the days of his life, and there shall no razor come upon his head. And it came to pass, as she continued praying before the Lord, that Eli marked her mouth. Now Hannah, she spake in her heart; only her lips moved, but her voice was not heard: therefore, Eli thought she had been drunken. And Eli said unto her, How long wilt thou be drunken? put away thy wine from thee. And Hannah answered and said, No, my lord, I am a woman of sorrowful spirit; I have drunk neither wine nor strong drink, but have poured out my soul before the Lord. Count not thine handmaid for a daughter of Belial: for out of the abundance of my complaint and grief have I spoken hitherto. Then Eli answered and said, Go in peace: and the God of Israel grant thee thy petition that thou hast asked of him" (I Samuel 1:6-17 KJV).

As you read the passage it is evident that Hannah was at a low place in her life. I can appreciate God's love for Hannah based on what she was going through and what she needed. God never bases our need for Him on the opinion of others. He comforts us in times of sorrow. The issues that are near to our hearts are near to His heart also.

Based upon personal experiences, I can tell you that I know God cares about even the smallest details of our lives. One instance, I prayed that God would make His plan clear regarding the university my oldest daughter was to attend. I wanted God to speak so loudly that even my youngest daughter would hear His voice. When her dad and I dropped her off at college, I thoroughly cleaned and decorated her room. We knew she had a balance of $7000. We didn't know how it would get paid, but my faith continued to soar. I reassured my daughter that God would provide. I reminded her that in the beginning we prayed, and God directed us, so I was sure He wouldn't allow us to fail. Even when her dad finally suggested she find a school closer to home, I stood in faith.

After we left her at the dorm, and crossed the state line on our way home, the Dean called me to inform me of a $6,000 scholarship for my daughter and they would also work with her on the remaining balance. Another time was during her second semester. She had a balance of $3,000. I did not have it, nor did I have access to it. I reminded her that God would provide as He did when she first moved into her dorm. Our faith was once again being tested, when she was notified via email that she needed to move out of her dorm by that following Sunday.

Once again, God does what He does best by showing us that He is concerned about us and those things that concern us. She received an email stating she was eligible for another scholarship because she made the Dean's List. If you would sit back and think for a moment, I am sure you can recall a time in which your back was against the wall and the only way out of that situation was through divine intervention. While it is not my goal to change anyone's belief system, I acknowledge the divine help that

He has given to us as a reminder that we matter to Him. The things that may appear as insignificant to man, are significant to Him. God's plans are not contingent upon man's perception.

When a woman goes into labor, the pain she feels seems unbearable, yet tolerable. She does not go into a fit and begin to throw herself around the room. Instead, she maintains a certain stable position to minimize the pain. As she gains stability in her position, she gets control of her breathing, thus making the pain manageable. Going with the flow of the pain gets her closer to the baby she has been preparing for.

Please allow me to clarify. Working against the pain increases the likelihood of severely scarred tissue. The damage is minimal when you are in stride versus going against the grain. When the baby is born, the mother does not focus on the pain she endured.

As hard as it may seem to believe, some good will come out of your pain. There is purpose in the pain. God is not the kind of God that would allow you to haphazardly endure affliction. If He allowed it, He has a greater purpose for it. Pain does not always yield bad results; it is the birthing place for a miracle to happen.

In the Bible, miracles never occurred during pleasant and perfect situations. You may know the story of the birth of Jesus and how He was conceived. His mother was engaged to be married to His father, yet Joseph and Mary never had sex. Joseph took his wife and left the city. They traveled to Bethlehem. Can you imagine… the Savior's parents basically living in hiding? They hid from the king who wanted Jesus killed because of the honor that was given to Him from those who knew who He was. Talk about a hardship! The birth of Jesus, [the Messiah of the world], was not the most convenient or pleasant birth.

My life has been anything but convenient. And I am a mother of "just five" children. I love using the term "just five" because it has special meaning to me. On the outside looking in, people see four or more children as a bad thing, especially for a single parent. But my children are my reason for everything. After all, it's "just five."

I can at least say that I did not give birth to my children in a distressed environment. I had a hospital bed to lay in until the birth of my children. Each of my children had their very own beds as well. Unlike our Redeemer, Jesus, He was born in an environment that was not conducive to a newborn baby or the mother, yet He is the Messiah.

I challenge you, from this day forward, to no longer downplay the circumstances you have survived. The pain is imperative to where God is taking you. Some things are solidified based on the circumstances endured. Despite where Jesus was born, the king wanted Him dead. Don't allow that place of inconvenience to overshadow the purpose for your life. The king did not care about the place of Jesus' birth; instead, the king was threatened by the purpose of Jesus. In the same way, the enemy is threatened by your purpose.

Even though my life was bad it could have been worse, my life had to remain within the confinement of God's will. The devil did not have free reign over my life. As in the story of Job, the enemy had to get permission from God to execute his demise against me.

> 'On another day the angels came to present themselves before the Lord, and Satan also came with them to present himself before him. And the Lord said to Satan, "Where have you come from?" Satan answered the Lord, "From roaming throughout the earth, going back and forth on it." Then the Lord said to Satan, "Have you considered my servant Job? There is no one on earth like him; he is blameless and upright, a man who fears God and shuns evil. And he still maintains his integrity, though you incited me against him to ruin him without any reason." "Skin for skin!" Satan replied. "A man will give all he has for his own life. But now stretch out your hand and strike his flesh and bones, and he will surely curse you to your face." The Lord said to Satan, "Very well, then, he is in your hands; but you must spare his life" (Job 2:1-6 NIV).

The enemy will launch an all-out attack to make you think that God is unaware of his tactics. Not only does God know about the enemy's plans for you, he had to consult God before his attempts. Focus on the fact that you are such a threat to the enemy, that he came against you in an infantile state. He could not wait until you had a chance to mature in God, he cheated and came against you when you could not defend yourself. It is much easier to dwell on the negative, but you should focus on the fact that you are "bad" (meaning good) in God and are a direct threat to the enemy! Everything you and I have encountered is because God knew you could handle it all and overcome.

Remember that God will not put more on us than we can bear, He doesn't haphazardly put us into danger, just as I would never in a million years leave my 15-year-old in charge of infant twins. I would not leave my 15-year-old daughter in charge because I know that she isn't mature enough to babysit them. And because of the love I have for them, I would never place them in a situation that would not be favorable to them.

We must understand how much God loves us. Because He loves us He would never allow us into a situation that would not be for our good and His glory. Although, many of the challenges we face are the results of our own disobedience, He does not find satisfaction in seeing you and I suffer. If our suffering can be used for a greater purpose, then rest assured He will allow it to happen. We must change our perspective on the difficulties we face in life as opportunities for growth.

CHAPTER 3

---ꙮ---

YOU NAME IT

Oftentimes, we miss the reason there is warfare over our lives. But rest assured, that nothing just happens! Nothing happens by mere accident or coincidence. For the majority of us, warfare is set in motion while we are in the womb.

God gave me a revelation about my name. My first name is Sarah, which biblically means "the mother of all nations." Contrarily, my middle name is Sapphira, which has a negative connotation—a wife that robbed God. The name is explained more in detail in the next chapter. The warfare over my life had very little to do with choices I've made. Instead, the warfare had everything to do with the war of good versus evil over the name that is tied to my destiny.

You must understand that when the enemy fights us, he is not after our current state, he fights us to keep us from fulfilling God's purpose over our lives. The enemy will use any and every opportunity he can to steer us from the path God originally has for us.

As we briefly look at the story of Ananias and Sapphira from the previous chapter, we will discover the motive was impure from the start. I do believe however, that Sapphira was led into disobedience by her loyalty to her husband, and please note that when I say, I believe there was something inside Sapphira that drove her disobedience, I am not defending her actions. I do believe the enemy took advantage of Sapphira, deceiving her into believing she and her husband would somehow be better off lying to the Holy Spirit and the Apostles.

Their story is found in Acts chapter 5, but if we read the previous chapter to gain proper understanding and background information, we will see that Ananias saw the generosity of Barnabas and noticed how please the Apostles were with what he'd done. Ananias wanted the honor without the true sacrifice and thus sought to manipulate the situation. Read the story below:

Chapter 4:36-37 states, *"And Joses, who by the apostles was surnamed Barnabas, (which is, being interpreted, The son of consolation,) a Levite, and of the country of Cyprus, Having land, sold it, and brought the money, and laid it at the apostles' feet."*

Chapter 5:1-4 reads, *"But a certain man named Ananias, with Sapphira his wife, sold a possession. And kept back part of the price, his wife also being privy to it, and brought a certain part, and laid it at the apostles' feet. But Peter said, Ananias, why hath Satan filled thine heart to lie to the Holy Ghost, and to keep back part of the price of the land? While it remained, was it not thine own? and after it was sold, was it not in thine own power? why hast thou conceived this thing in thine heart? thou hast not lied unto men, but unto God."*

I shared this story to show you the story behind the name of Sapphira. For those that may be saying, "It is just a name" and asking, "Does it really matter?" Yes, it does. Your name speaks to your destiny. There are a few occasions in which people's names were changed. Assuming names have no significant meaning, there would be no point in God changing the name of Saul to Paul, Jacob to Israel, Abram to Abraham, Sarai to Sarah or Simon to Peter. It would be safe to say the new name spoke to the place God was taking them.

It also depicts the reality of their old name that also spoke contrary to God's will for their lives. There is power in a name. As children of the Most-High God, we are wonderfully created in His image. And since we are born in the image of God, we have the same benefits as our Father.

I have no doubt that my mother did not intend to give me a name with a horrible meaning. She simply chose something from the Bible that she thought was beautiful. But that is also what the enemy does, he plays on our lack of knowledge. Glory to God, despite what the enemy means for evil, God makes it work for our good. As Genesis 1:27 tells us, God created us in His own image. So regardless of what is attached to our names, God has fashioned us after Himself.

Jesus has the name above every other name in heaven and on earth. The name of Jesus is powerful. Not only is His name powerful, but everything in the universe has to respond to His name. My name and your name set the tone and speak to the God-given destiny over our lives. Since we are created in the image of God, our names have effect over everything around us.

It's unfortunate that we serve a great God, but limit what the Word of God says about us and the authority He has given us because of our image in Him. Now, if demons tremble at the name of Jesus, and we have the same authority that Jesus has, then what more can we expect with our names? I am not saying that demons tremble at the sound of our names, however, I am saying that our names cause a ripple effect in the atmosphere.

My oldest daughter, Faith, is constantly reminded that she is not to be moved by what she sees. Therefore, she has learned to not respond to unfavorable situations. I have explained to her the reason that I named her Faith was because of the difficulties I faced while pregnant with her. I literally forced myself to believe better would happen despite the doctor's diagnosis.

After taking a sonogram, the doctor's discovered that my placenta was trying to detach itself from the wall of my uterus. To sum it up to the best of my ability, the placenta was trying to unplug from the wall that was keeping the sac in place. If the sac got out of place, it could have resulted in a miscarriage.

I did not allow my emotions to get the best of me. Instead, I spoke life over my baby, Faith. And by the grace of God, I carried her full term of 40 weeks. She weighed a healthy 8 pounds and 11 ounces! I am convinced that her name helped me to speak life over her and thus birth her full term.

Let's review the story of Abraham in the Bible: In spite of his old age, Abraham's name carried weight in the spirit. As a result of the weight of his name that was connected to God's promises for Abraham's life, it was imperative for Abraham to conceive a child in his old age. When God gives you a promise, it does not matter what it looks like around you, or who believes with you for the promise, you can rest assured that the promise will come to pass. The enemy knows this, so his plans are to get you and I so focused on what we do not have instead on what is coming. You and I must be cognizant of the fact that the enemy knows he has no power to abort God's plan in our lives; however, he can cause us to abort and walk away from those things that God desires to do in and through us. The enemy relies on you and I not knowing God's plan for our lives and anticipates our unbelief and wavering back and forth regarding those things God desires to do.

God created man to duplicate Him. It matters that you and I mimic his authority and suffering. Many can identify with the sharing in the sufferings of Christ, while neglecting the authority He walked in. Things happened because of the words He spoke. The enemy expects for you and I to walk in His sufferings and forget to walk in His authority. The conflict began in the natural with my name and became a catalyst for spiritual complications. The Word tells us that things first occur in the natural realm, then the spiritual realm. As situations unfold in the natural realm, something begins to unfold in the spiritual realm.

> "Howbeit that was not first which is spiritual, but that which is natural; and afterward that which is spiritual"
> —(1 Corinthians 15:46 KJV)

I am sure my mother's intentions for me were good. However, good intentions do not exempt an individual from ignorant behavior or the consequences that follow. It's not enough to have thoughts of doing good, they must be backed up by our actions. And, considering that there are no manuals on how to be a perfect parent, people will make mistakes. There are also many factors to consider, such as whether or not there is a two-parent home? Or if the child was planned versus a teen pregnancy?

I believe my mother did the very best she could with the information and resources that were made available to her. I am very thankful that my mother decided to keep me and not abort me.

I challenge you to rejoice over being a "kept baby" by your biological parents, as well as a "kept baby" by your Heavenly Father. My mother's love for me was great. However, my Heavenly Father had even greater plans for my life.

Oftentimes, we forget that our Heavenly Father is more concerned with the outcome of our lives than our biological parents. We make the mistake of believing our "dark paths" are because we are not God's priority. The love of your Heavenly Father supersedes the love of your parents. After all, it was His plan for your parent's paths to connect and later conceive. Your Heavenly Father knew you before conception. Your Heavenly Father loved the thought of you before you were conceived. Your parents lacked this ability. Your parents could only begin to love the thought of you from the moment they were aware of conception.

God's love for you is demonstrated through faith. This perspective does not diminish a parents' love, but it is designed to show that we have a Heavenly Father who is more concerned about us and our lives. This perspective should bring peace and acceptance to your soul... just to know you were more than a heartbeat to your Heavenly Father. It is your choice as to how you choose to look at the glass half full instead of half empty.

> "For I know the plans I have for you, declares the Lord, plans to prosper you and not harm you, plans to give you hope and a future"
> —(Jeremiah 29:11 NIV)

As a new creation in Christ, we do not have to lose hope. You can choose to live a defeated life, or you can choose to count your blessings and keep moving forward. I am not negating the difficulties that you've faced. But you do not have to stay there. There are many things you have that someone else may lack at this very moment. Count your blessings, considering the things you have been exposed to. You may not have grown up in a palace, but God still has a plan for you.

I would not focus much on how things used to be. As you yield to the process that God has chosen to get you where He wants you to be, you will discover that God compensates for inconveniences in our lives when we wholeheartedly decide to follow and obey Him and His ways. Whatever you do, do not allow situations to cause you to forfeit the will of God for your life. Do not allow your desires to overpower God's desires for your life. When we are in alignment with God's plan and purpose for our lives, He will give us the desires of our heart. Disobedience and our lust will cause us to seek those things that are contrary to God's word. But He reminds us in Psalms 37:4 to delight ourselves in Him, and He will give us the desires of our hearts.

> "Though thy beginning was small, yet thy latter end should greatly increase"
> —(Job 8:7 KJV)

A glass of water is a glass of water, regardless of the location. The only difference in the glass of water is the perception of the individual that is about to consume the water. An individual who just finished eating a bag of chips may perceive the glass as being half empty. On the other hand, an individual who may not be thirsty may perceive the glass as being half full. Your environment creates your perception, whether good or bad.

Take a moment to examine your perception. I had to examine my perception of the name Sarah (the mother of all nations) versus Sapphira (cheater, liar against God). By default, I gravitated to my first name because it was positive.

Did I wake up one morning and say, "I think I will just live my life this way?" Not at all. Every individual can gravitate toward good or evil but not both simultaneously.

The God of the universe was drawing me in the direction that would bring Him glory in my life. It is not a coincidence that I have five children and I love each of my children very much. I would not trade their lives for anything.

Did I dream of having five children? No, I wanted two children because I did not want to experience the pain of childbirth. As a child, I was constantly reminded of how intolerable giving birth would be. The source of that information never mentioned that there were medical drugs to reduce and numb the pain. I decided that having two children was best based on the information that I perceived as truth. God knew that I would need all five of my children and He knew I would be the perfect fit to be their mother. God knew there would be times in my life I would literally want to give up, but during those times my children became my inspiration for living. That does not mean I am a perfect mom. Neither does it mean I did everything right as a mother. God knew He could trust me with my children's lives to pray over them and to commit them back to Him.

We must be careful not to allow the things that do not make sense to us, hinder the move of God in our lives. My children and I were residents at two domestic abuse shelters for women. We were forced to leave and return to the place where we were abused. This happened because I made the mistake in sharing my location with my mother. For those of you who are not familiar with the rules of a shelter for battered women and children, one of the rules is that you do not share your location with anyone. And although it was a rule violation, it was my mother, so I didn't see the harm in telling her. She shared the information with my sister who repeated the information to my son's father. I only shared the information with her because she was very worried about us and I didn't want her to worry. I tried to reassure her that we were well, and I went ahead and told her that we were at the shelter. I wanted her to know the truth, so I also gave her the location of the shelter.

During that time my son's father and I were also in the middle of a custody battle. I received a call from my attorney informing me that the plaintiff's attorney called and told them if I wanted to retain custody of my son that I needed to return to my home. I felt as though I had no choice, but to return. From that day forward, I knew and understood what it meant to not have support and loyalty from family. My mother shared my location with my sister and my sister wasn't concerned about our well-being, she shared our location with my son's father. After being kicked out of the shelter and nowhere else to turn, I returned to the place of my abuser.

Initially, he did not want us to live there, but allowed us back. After repeatedly sharing with him that I was no longer on the pill, he forced himself on me. We wrestled from our bedroom to the bathroom and finally ended up tussling in the closet, which is where the violation took place. As a result of that rape, my twins were conceived. I had mixed feelings concerning the pregnancy after the rape by my husband. In addition to the horrific ordeal of being raped, I had to face the looks of so-called friends that were told I tricked him into getting me pregnant.

I never had the opportunity to share what really happened. I was baffled at the thought of people perceiving that I'd manipulate him into getting me pregnant. I was the one who left and wanted out of the abusive situation. When I finally decided to leave with my kids, grabbing birth control pills was the last thing on my mind. My concern was our safety.

Neither repairing my marriage nor being intimate with anyone else was a concern for me, therefore, I did not think it would be a big deal for me to have them. I thought nothing else of the matter.

When I received the phone call from my attorney, the thought never crossed my mind that I was no longer on the pill. My initial thought was to follow his instructions, so that I could maintain custody of my son.

It took me a long time to release the guilt that was placed on me from people who had no clue of what happened. It took me a long time to hold my head up despite what others said. I had to see myself in the truth of being a rape victim. The fact that he was my husband on paper did not justify his actions. After carrying that guilt and shame, I later discovered it was my self-perception that carried more weight.

It is not too late to change how you view yourself. Yes, you may have made some really bad decisions. Guess what? Those decisions do not define you as an individual. Neither do those decisions define where you are going. However, the fact that you beat the odds of the statistics against you, your strength and tenacity have been highlighted.

You are defined as a survivor of every obstacle you overcame. You have the right to believe, write and rewrite the script for your life. Let's begin with choosing those things that are good and of good report. Choose wisely and carefully.

CHAPTER 4

IT'S NOT YOUR CHOICE

You may not have a negative connotation attached to your name, but you are a survivor! No one survivor is greater than another survivor. A survivor of cancer carries the same weight as a survivor of domestic violence. All survivors carry the same character trait…they refuse to remain in the corner. To the survivor, some movement is better than no movement at all. Therefore, it is wise to avoid prejudging others. You are not privy to the trials they are facing to keep their sanity. The best thing you can do for that individual is to pray that God would increase their strength during their process. No one is exempt from challenges or hardships of any kind; everyone must have a valley experience. A valley experience is any experience that causes you to question your purpose and why you are experiencing some form of difficulty. A valley experience can also be equivalent to having a "thorn in the flesh." A "thorn in the flesh" keeps you humble.

Some of you reading this book have survived multiple things, meaning you have endured more than your fair share of difficulties. Life has dealt you several bad hands, but you are still standing. You may have a few scars from the pain, but you made it through. Don't allow your insecurities to cause you to become stuck. Although scars are evident, so are signs of victory. Every time you overcome the hindrances in your life, you are given a hat of victory that says "that" situation did not overtake you. Yes, you may have wanted to quit, but it did not defeat you. Defeat was not your crown, there were some character traits that were developed and served to strengthen you. Warriors are developed in battles. If you have encountered battle after battle, you, my friend, are being perfected as a warrior.

When David fought the bear and the lion, he was being prepared for his next battle with Goliath. But he wasn't prepared for King Saul. David said he could have taken it better if Saul was his enemy, but Saul was like a father to him, therefore, he dealt with Saul using wisdom.

> "And David said unto Saul, Thy servant kept his father's sheep, and there came a lion, and a bear, and took a lamb out of the flock: And I went out after him, and smote him, and delivered it out of his mouth: and when he arose against me, I caught him by his beard, and smote him, and slew him, Thy servant slew both the lion and the bear: and this uncircumcised Philistine shall be as one of them, seeing he hath defied the armies of the living God. David said moreover, The Lord that delivered me out of the paw of the lion, and out of the paw of the bear, he will deliver me out of the hand of this Philistine. And Saul said unto David, Go, and the Lord be with thee" (1 Samuel 17:34-37 KJV).

David could have complained about his encounter with the trouble he faced. Complaining about his trouble would not have prepared him for what was to come in his immediate future. Consider thinking and breathing outside of what you know to be familiar. Perhaps what you are going through this very instance has absolutely nothing to do with you. What you are going through may be about a divine appointment you will have with an individual.

Only God knows what we need to prepare us for the next level. He allows situations for the betterment of His plan in our lives. Can you imagine the order of events that would have transpired if David had not submitted to the process of defeating the bear and the lion? He would not have been prepared to defeat the giant, Goliath.

If David had not defeated the bear and lion, he would not have been convinced that the size of the giant was not a factor. David would have gotten stuck on the impossibilities of him defeating a bear and a lion. It is not God's will for you to become stifled in the level of attack that He has allowed. Focus on the previous battles that ended victoriously and allow those reference points to serve as reminders of His faithfulness.

Often time, many of us, at one point or another, do not see ourselves the way God sees us. We will "dumb down" our perception of self as we make the mistake of comparing ourselves to others. Our DNA is made known to Him and He selects the individuals that are capable in Him to execute His plan and purpose here on earth. Trust that God knows your DNA. Trust God and His plans for your life. For a moment, compare God's plan for your life to that of a nursing student in an undergraduate program. Although the focus may be on health, the non-core classes are equally important to the development of an academic year as a nursing student. As a current student, you may never understand the importance of the variety of classes that are required for graduation. It is not until the nursing student has completed the program before he or she can fully understand the importance of the variety of classes. If the nursing student acts prematurely by withdrawing from the nursing program, they will never experience the freedom of completion and the ability to provide for his or her family.

The story of your life will end victoriously, provided you do not throw in the towel and call it quits, simply because of something you may not understand or agree with. Just like the nursing student, you too must learn the importance of why God allowed certain things to transpire in your life. Don't abort the freedom that comes with completion and submission. Continue to walk away from "the quitting and rebellious spirit" that yields an unwanted harvest of lack.

CHAPTER 5

GROOMED TO DO IT

Before he was King, David was in his own world as he tended the sheep. David did not initially pursue the lion, bear or the giant. Instead, God chose the situations that would best groom David for greatness. Regardless of your pedigree, anointing, or prominence, God does not allow individuals to choose their own grooming process. Grooming is defined by Merriam Webster as readiness or preparedness for a specific objective. Biblically, we can also call it "pruning". Pruning comes in many facets—even through battle. It is a painful but necessary process. The bible tells us our light affliction does not compare with the greater glory we are to receive. Therefore, we can miss the beauty of being a survivor, if we only focus on the battle.

God gives us an open book test. We have His Word and that gives us the artillery that we need to win each war. Although we have a common enemy, we still do not know each tactic he will use in warring against us. We can fight from an offensive and defensive position in Christ.

When given the diagnosis of cancer on my vocal cords, I cried a little bit and immediately began to say what the Word of God said about me, my life and my health. I did not focus on the cancer nor the people I felt should have been there for me. Instead, I focused on being healed and being a model for God's glory, healing power, and grace. God did not cause the cancer. However, He allowed it for a greater purpose than the intent of the enemy. The sickness was not unto death, but unto the Glory of God. He was grooming me to do life differently.

I fought defensively, using everything at my disposal. My defensive artillery included sowing sacrificial seeds, repeating the Word of God, positive affirmations, praise and worship, prayer, selective colors of clothing that expressed positive affirmation, and I implemented the suggestions made by my nutritionist to improve my overall well-being.

There were times my throat was too sore to talk, drink, or swallow sips of water. Even though I was restricted in my own voice, I was still going to worship God. Even if it meant using the voice of another to create an atmosphere that would be conducive to my healing. I knew a spirit-filled atmosphere would also serve to counterattack the plans of the enemy. During this intense "grooming process," I began to play Dr. Cindy Trimm's Spiritual Warfare Prayer CD. I understood the power of prayer and saturated my environment by any means necessary. I know that it was only through God's grace that I endured what seemed like one thing after another.

Despite what you may be facing today, no matter how bad things may be, you have something left that can be used. All is not lost. All within the same year, literally within five months, I received a diagnosis of cancer, faced divorce and buried my father. I had many things I could have used to help me cope, but regardless of what I faced,

I chose God in every process. The process was not easy, but I had grown accustomed to declaring each day, "I AM A SURVIVOR." I had one choice, and that was to come out victorious. Dying and leaving my children motherless was not an option. Being bitter during the legal process of the divorce and afterwards was not an option. Living in grief after the death of my father was not an option. Surviving was my only option.

The grooming process will catapult you into your purpose. Unknowingly, everything that I encountered was working for my good. God proved Himself my Victor repeatedly. I had no reason to doubt Him. God brought me through some tumultuous situations that others thought I would not overcome. But being the risk taker that I am, I was desperate enough to believe every word God said about me. I held on to every word for dear life!

I challenge you to let go of every word that has been spoken against you, over you and to you. Do not allow those words of death to resonate in your spirit. One of the oldest tricks the enemy uses is for you and me to discredit the good that God has already done in our lives. One strategy I continue to use to this day is to play reverse psychology with the devil. I am referring to not allowing what you feel to reflect on the outside.

Often, when I am feeling my worst, I will go to the extreme to make sure my makeup is on point and I am looking my absolute best. I know many see this as a mask, but it is really me prophesying to myself. It is a prophetic act to say, "My best days are right in front of me."

I am determined to never allow the enemy to see me sweat. Even though I had every right to feel down, I would not succumb to those feelings. I wanted to make sure that I was living according to God's plans and not my feelings.

You may want to give up, but don't you dare announce it publicly. Not announcing it does not imply that you are in denial, instead you simply refuse to supply the enemy with ammunition to later assassinate you.

Make the devil tired of his failed plans and plots against you. Do not comply with his evil assignment. If you give in or throw in the towel you are doing exactly that. If you've spoken those words, you can only change them by renouncing them. And from this point forward, take positive actions that will produce better results.

God is looking for a yielded vessel to demonstrate His glory. If no one is sick, how can God be known as a Healer? If no one experiences financial lack, how can God be known as a Provider? If no one has been disappointed, how can God be known as a Comforter?

All throughout the Bible, healing manifestations of the presence of God and deliverances came by way of the people. Do not allow your circumstances to cause you to succumb to an all-time low mentally. You are a force to be reckoned with. The enemy knows who you were designed to be in God's plan and purpose, and that is why he started his evil plot against you at an early age.

Change your perspective about the harsh realities and embrace the fact that you have been chosen by God. Whatever your "grooming process" looks like, it will all work for you and not against you.

> "And we know that all things work together for good to them that love God, to them who are the called according to his purpose"
> — (Romans 8:28 KJV)

Your "grooming process" will often validate the call upon your life and enable you to utilize your God given potential to help and encourage others. Pain has no face. Pain has no color. Pain has feelings, and it is through the association of pain that many reading this book can relate to every word. The Bible tells us at Hebrews 4:15, that we do not have a High Priest who cannot sympathize with us in our hour of weakness because He was tempted [endured] everything that we must endure.

Pain, rejection, abandonment and betrayal are things our Heavenly Father endured during His time as He walked the earth to His crucifixion. That connects Him to us as our Savior.

> "For we do not have a High Priest who is unable to sympathize and understand our weaknesses and temptations, but One who has been tempted [knowing exactly how it feels to be human] in every respect as we are, yet without [committing any] sin"
> —(Hebrews 4:15 AMP)

Some people spend excessive amounts of time upset over the absence of people in their lives. What if it was more beneficial that they did not have an active share in your life? What if God had a greater purpose? If a person does not pursue a relationship with us, we have the proclivity to automatically assume the worse. Perhaps your father or mother were absent from your life, and as a result, you grew up resenting them for not being there for you; you must see it through different lenses. In some cases, God restores the broken relationships, but even if He doesn't, you must know that God will never leave nor forsake you.

Consider also, if your parents had caused more damage than good by being an active part of your life? Yes, we can assume that all parents are responsible in their actions. Yes, we can assume that perhaps they should have known better than to bring a child into the world and not provide the love needed for the child. Going back and forth is not productive or conducive to the vitality of your mental health.

At some point, you must accept the hand that life has dealt you. Taking ownership of those things that have happened, does not imply that you agree with the circumstances, it simply means that you acknowledge your truth. As you acknowledge your truth, you must also release them from your expectations of accountability. This will give you inner peace. Getting to that place of peace equips you with the power to relinquish any pain that you are holding on to.

If you hold on to the matter, you literally delay the inner healing that will come forth from the release. You can choose to wallow in self-pity and think you've missed a whole lot, or you can accept the choices that were beyond your control. You can also choose to think on things that are conducive to positivity and purpose. Sometimes individuals are so devastated over the mental and emotional trauma that the wrong person caused them, that they are unwilling to gravitate toward those that God purposed for their lives. Wipe the dust from your face and get back up emotionally and mentally and embrace the people God has assigned to your life.

While everyone cannot make a deposit into your life, everyone should not be turned away. No one can tell you who should no longer remain and those that should stay. That's a decision only you can make. At the appointed time, God will reveal to you those individuals that are a part of the subtraction and addition team. Everyone is born with the ability to hear and listen with their heart. Trust your inner voice.

CHAPTER 6

DIVINE TIMING

As I sat on a plane for my dream vacation to Hawaii, there was a group that sat behind me complaining of the pilot's late arrival. They complained by saying things like passengers do not have the luxury of having pilots wait if they are running late for their flights, and we shouldn't have to be inconvenienced because the pilot has a delay. I thought their conversation was a bit skewed and limited. The truth of the matter is that prior to taking my flight in case of impending danger, I prayed for a divine delay.

When the pilot announced that there would be a delay, I immediately wondered what God was protecting us from. I also wanted a seat closer to the front of the plane, but then I heard the voice of the Lord say, "Stay in the seat you have been assigned." I whispered, "Okay."

In addition to the delayed flight, I was unable to finalize my scheduled transportation from the airport to my hotel. But there was a family that lived in the area that was traveling the same direction. We greeted one another, made small talk, and the mother of the group confirmed the expensive cost for shuttle transportation. She worked next door to the hotel resort of my lodging and offered me a ride to my resort. Her words were, "You can keep the $66 that you would have paid for shuttle transportation.

There are seven of us, and we can make room for you to ride with us."

Not only does God provide, but His plans are not equal to our plans; neither are His thoughts equal to our thoughts. Meanwhile, we can align our thoughts and plans to be in sync with His. There is a difference between alignment and being equal. To be equal indicates that the levels are the same. And alignment indicates agreement or alliance.

When we are improperly aligned, we can mistakenly think that God is supposed to be in sync with us, and not us in sync with Him. As a result, we can make decisions prematurely, and move ahead of God, and cause delays that could have been avoided.

Not all delays are divine; when we allow ourselves to become impatient and complain about the lack of speed in our lives, then it is safe to say that most of us are in situations this very moment because we grew weary in waiting on God's plans to manifest. Let's face it, many of us miss God by moving ahead of His timing. But even in that, He is still faithful to meet us in our time of distress.

Although, God will meet us, He usually does not move as quickly as we would like for Him to. He will allow us to learn the lessons from the situations that we've created. Refusing to learn from our mistakes will cause us to repeat the same things over again. Instead of repeating mistakes, allow the lessons learned to change the trajectory of your life.

As difficult as it may sound, take a moment and reflect on the setbacks and delays you have encountered, and look for God in those situations. You will know if and when you have experienced a divine delay or setback by the result of the outcome. Was the outcome of delay favorable to you? Some delays in our lives are allowed and ordained by God for His purpose.

When I experience delays it is an opportunity for me to hit the reset button in my life. An opportunity to look at my life and be honest with myself and examine how I landed in a situation that was not advantageous for me. Needing a reset allows you to take inventory of your life. Once you have an inventory of your life, you are better equipped to make the necessary changes. When we make the necessary adjustments to come into alignment with God's plan, there will be acceleration in our lives. The flight for my trip should have taken five hours nonstop. But the pilot announced there would be an early landing to The Big Island!

Most of us have heard of Noah's Ark as children, if not, it is found in the bible at Genesis chapters 6 and 7. Noah was commissioned by God to build an ark for the preservation of his family and those who trusted the Word of God. Review it in your spare time.

Can you imagine what the world that we know would be like if Noah did not come into alignment with God's plan? After careful study of Noah's mandate to build the ark, perhaps you are pondering what would have happened if he failed to do as God instructed? We can be grateful that he chose to agree with God's plans.

Just as God allowed the flood in Noah's day, you may not understand why God has allowed certain things to happen in your life, but when you know the heart of God and the character of God, you ultimately know that God's plan does not include destruction for your life. The fact that you are still here indicates that God is not finished with you. You cannot focus on what your current situation looks like. Remember, what is around you may be a total contradiction of where you are going. Your current situation does not define you. Instead, your current situation will serve as the birthing ground for tenacity. What is strength if it is not birthed out of adversity? What is tenacity if it is not birthed out of enduring countless moments where you wanted to give up?

Some people are born with a tenacious attitude and for many of us, it is developed through hardship and crisis. I love the analogy where tenacity is compared to a Pit bull. Pit bulls are described as being determined and strong-willed by nature. Make no apologies for having a pit bull mentality. By the same token, there are many people who wish they had this character trait. And often will admire your resolve to stand in the face of adversity.

Noah stood against the grain and built the ark when others thought he was insane. Noah was so determined to obey God that he continued to build when building was not popular. Are you willing to follow hard after the desires God has given you? You must be willing to achieve each desire with everything that is within you, at all cost. Don't allow "at all cost" to intimidate you.

Your focus should be so centered on completing each goal at hand. Yes, it will be hard but so is living a life you've never desired for yourself. Living beneath your best self is to deny and diminish your potential. There is a price that must be paid for success of any kind. To achieve optimal results, you must decide to win.

No one said things would be easy. In the meantime, if someone says it is easy, you may want to run far, far away from that liar!

When I look over my life and the achievements I have accomplished, I am amazed of the inner strength I never knew I possessed. As I face new challenges, I am often reminded of each previous encounter of struggle and victory. I strongly believe that you cannot have victory without a struggle.

The struggle should serve as a thorn in our flesh that is a constant reminder of all that we have encountered, endured and overcame. The struggle should never set us in the direction of defeat. Get a grip on the struggles you face today.

YOU HAVE THE ABILITY TO TAKE CONTROL OF EACH STRUGGLE!

If you were to examine the lives of natural born survivors, you will find they are content with their portion of life. The disadvantage of wanting another person's life is the uncertainty of the God-given grace for the desired life. Just because someone's life appears to be grand, does not mean it is void of trouble. No matter how rough your life has been, God has equipped you with mercy daily. Someone else may look at your life and wonder how you survived the embarrassment. You survived simply because He gave you new mercies. God is such a loving Father that He gives us what we need for each step that we are on. Each person has tailor made grace and mercy. What I need, may be vastly different from what the next person needs.

> "And he said unto me, My grace is sufficient for thee: for my strength is made perfect in weakness"
> —(2 Corinthians 12:9 KJV)

The unmerited favor that has been given to you, enables you to go through seasons of lack, uncertainty, sickness and losses. God's grace proves our dependence upon Him. Grace does not negate the mishaps you have experienced, instead grace gives you the ability to "do it" when you don't understand "how you did it."

While it is not my intention to negate the struggles you have encountered, I want you to think about the many individuals you will be empowered to reach because of your pain. Remember, you cannot reach people and be effective if you have not gone through the dark places of pain that many have visited.

Each of us can pursue the perfect will (His desire) for our lives or His permissive will (what He allows). When we venture out and embrace the path that He has not ordained for us, we endure things He never wanted us to endure. It is important to stop right where you are, and take an assessment of your location spiritually, emotionally and physically and begin to trace your steps. I assure you that you did not get to where you are overnight. It will take more than overnight to get you back to the place God wants you to be.

During your assessment, it is imperative that you be honest with how you got to the place that you are in. Be sure to list the inadequacies, deficiencies, and the insecurities. It is essential that you identify the weaknesses in your life. As you access your weaknesses, you will gain insight regarding why you made certain decisions. Don't be too hard on yourself, introspection is helpful. No one wakes up and decides to make a bad decision. Instead, there are always a series of events that were the catalyst of their "why?" Unfortunately, without realizing it many people make decisions from the place of pain.

When my father passed away, I had to come to grips with the things that I would never experience with him. For starters, I have never sat on my father's lap. My father never held me in his arms. It was painful for me to accept this truth. So, I had to be brutally honest with myself when it came to men. When I began to have feelings of abandonment and rejection, I had to articulate how I felt and what current actions triggered those feelings from the past.

As I began to take inventory of this area in my life, I understood my negative reactions and behaviors. It caused me to be cognizant of my actions and feelings. Instead of continuing in the pattern of destruction, I adopted a different way of thinking. Changing my thoughts led to alternative behaviors that were more productive toward my healing. And allowed me to vent my frustrations in a place of safety. If I avoided introspection, I would have continued down the dark path of not understanding why I did certain things. Failing to uncover those deeply rooted pains often leads people in continuous despair.

You also want to identify the strengths. You may be wondering, "How is it possible for an individual's strength to cause them to get off track?" Sometimes strength is a mask for pain. A person may be independent and may get ahead of God by pursuing something that God never ordained for their lives.

Rejection is often displayed in overachieving. And this can lead to pride. Thus, a person must learn to be independent under the guidance of his or her dependence on God.

In reassessing goals that were once dear to my heart, I learned to evaluate what was more important. Was it more important to pursue my dream of being an attorney while my children suffer as a result of me not being there, or pursue the dream of being a great mother to the children God ordained me to teach and guide? The pursuit of dreams does not have to die. Rearranging the order of the pursuit of those dreams is an art that many never get the chance to master.

Things happened and it is okay to put a dream on hold. Please do not confuse putting a dream on hold with compromising your dream for the sake of another individual. Even the Word of God tells us to be equally yoked. All throughout the Old Testament, there are countless stories of how it was forbidden to marry outside of your tribe or "kind." To stay within your kind implies a harmony that may not exist if you search outside the realm of familiarity. I've been humbled and learned a lot from three failed marriages. I often put my goals on hold to pursue "love" relationships. And discovered those pursuits were not always what God ordained for my life.

The key here is to remain under the umbrella of God's protection and to be in sync with the mind of God. Many create havoc for their own lives simply because they choose their own path instead of the path that He has for them. Stay in your lane and want only those things and friendships that God desires to give you. The Word tells us, "to delight ourselves in Him and He shall give thee the desires of thine heart" (Psalm 37:4).

The only way that can manifest into our lives is when we come into alignment with God's plans and desires for us. If we do not come into alignment with His plans, then we are coveting what belongs to Satan, which ultimately ends in destruction. God is under no obligation to manifest those things in our lives that are centered on coveted prayers.

CHAPTER 7

YOURS, NOT THEIRS

As you remain in your lane, keep in mind, it is your lane. So do not expect mom, dad, sister, best friend or spouse to get on board with you. People you love the most may not be equipped to take you to the places God has ordained for you to go. People, including those who have a special place in your heart, will only allow you to go as far as their minds will allow you to conceive. People cannot take you to places they have yet to visit themselves.

Refuse to be bound by the limitations that others may attempt to place on you. People limit you for a variety of reasons; one may be because they are limited in their own thinking and faith. Second, because they may not wish to see you prosper. As much as you may love them, if they hinder your progress, consider separating yourself for a season.

The adage, "birds of a feather flock together," holds a truth that we can apply to our lives. The moment you realize you are not going in the same direction of those around you, you owe it to yourself to change your circle of influence. After all, we become the company we keep. Unconsciously, we "fail" when we choose to continue to associate ourselves with individuals that have become complacent in negativity and are going absolutely "nowhere."

It is not that you have mastered this thing called life, it's just insane to continue doing things the way you have done them and expect there to be change. Change your circle of association and watch your life change.

In Galatians, you will find a description of Paul's experience once he acknowledged God calling him to His purpose. Before Paul's conversion, he was treacherous towards the people of God. It is safe to say that Paul was the modern-day Isis of his time. Paul stayed in his lane of what God had called him to do. He did not go to the other apostles and tell them of the things God was doing and had spoken in his life.

Instead, Paul obediently followed God as He separated him to prepare him for the journey ahead. Paul embraced his time of isolation.

Many people desire their "next" without the isolation. To experience the "next" without isolation is to miss the one on one training by God. Paul spent three years in Arabia more than likely unlearning much of what he learned at the time he hated and murdered Christians. As we learned in an early chapter, God must purge us to purify us.

> *"But when it pleased God, who separated me from my mother's womb, and called me by his grace, to reveal his Son in me, that I might preach him among the heathen; immediately I conferred not with flesh and blood: neither went I up to Jerusalem to them which were apostles before me; but I went into Arabia, and returned again unto Damascus"* (Galatians 1:15-17).

While on my dream vacation in Hawaii, the weather began to change and suddenly a tropical storm was headed to The Big Island. I prayed over the trip and everything concerning the trip before the date I arrived. I was confident in the fact that God had answered my prayer of protection.

After trusting God for six weeks of radiation going into my body, I was positive that God was more than capable of keeping me safe while on the island.

Despite the turn of events, God knew I would be vacationing at precisely the time the meteorologist predicted a tropical storm. As a daughter of the Most High, it is not His desire for us to be driven by fear. When we are driven by fear, God is not in the midst.

> "For God has not given us the spirit of fear; but of power, and of love, and a sound mind"
> —(2 Timothy 1:7 KJV)

It takes more energy to think of all the things that could go wrong. Therefore, instead of using my energy negatively, I chose to believe God. To me, the cancer diagnosis was no different than the tropical storm headed my way. This is what I like to call "blind faith." You really can't see your way through, but like the pit bull that refuses to surrender his bone, you refuse to let go of God's Word.

No matter how the situation may look that you are currently facing, find what the Word of God has to say concerning it and speak it over your life. For example, during the time of radiation treatments, I knew I wanted to be healed, and I searched for every scripture concerning healing and declared them over my body. Taking God at His Word, caused a shift to take place in my life. That shift attracted the thing I desired the most, which was healing.

The day I received the cancer diagnosis, I began to educate myself as much as possible. I was determined to not be at the mercy of the doctors and rely on everything they said to me.

I continued my workout at the gym and did not water down my workouts based on the cancer treatments. God demonstrated His power and strength through my body. Based on what the doctors and nutritionist said, I should not have been able to physically maintain my workout. I knew that it was not enough for me to say what God said about my healing and not be willing to add the works; I had to take the steps toward optimal health—exercising, eating right, taking my supplements, and positive affirmations. I mentioned how intentional I was about the colors I wore. I didn't wear blacks or grays, instead I wore vibrant colors to reflect life.

The worst decision anyone can make when they receive bad news is the decision to crawl into a hole and wait to die. Dead things crawl into holes to officiate their very own memorial service! As long as you have breath in your body, you are alive. So live!

If you are a natural born fighter, then you have been chosen by God as an intercessor. You may be asking…how did you conclude God has called me as an intercessor? You have survived the dark places and know exactly how to pray for others in similar dark places. To help reach and encourage someone else, you must be willing to allow God to write your story for His glory.

We can place limitations on ourselves and others. So what, if you are ripe in age? God has not changed His mind about you. Imagine having a baby like Sarah at the age of 95? God made good on His promise! So what if you have more than one "baby daddy?" God has not changed His mind about you. Abraham had three "baby mommas," and God still fulfilled His promises. So, what if you have been an outcast? Joseph was an outcast among his own brothers, yet God used him to deliver his own family during a time of famine.

Although you may have been conceived out of wedlock, God has a plan for your life. The words and actions of death that were meant to destroy you could not penetrate the life God has spoken over you. Right now, your enemies are in awe you are still alive. Some of them have burned candles and prayed against the very air you breathe. Despite the attempts of the enemy to kill you prematurely, there is a greater force working on your behalf. Legions of angels were assigned to you at birth. When you fight, you are not fighting alone. The fight has been fixed. You cannot lose.

> "What shall we then say to these things? If God be for us, who can be against us?"
> —(Romans 8:31 KJV)

God fights for us! It is when we do not understand this truth that we succumb to a victim mentality. Not only does God love you, but He has also sent you assistance, there are angels warring, guarding, and protecting you. Baby girl, God has preserved you for such a time as this. Dear Sir, God has great need of you.

Due to the pain you have endured, you will attract other fighters to you. They may not understand why they are attracted to you. Take each lesson learned as a gold medal from your Heavenly Father. Gold medals are not just given, one must earn them. Furthermore, gold medals are not given in potato sack races, instead, gold medals are given in extreme testing conditions.

Each challenge you have faced, has prepared and propelled you into the next challenge. Reference points also serve as reminders… whatever it is that you may be facing, it too shall pass. There is a season for everything. No one season can last forever. I am reminded of God's promise of my latter days being better than my former days.

> "Though thy beginning was small, yet thy latter end should greatly increase"
> —(Job 8:7)

The above Scripture is an anchor in my soul. Not only does it mean things will get better, but I will have no reference point in this place. The place of latter cannot be compared to anything I have already experienced. This latter place is more than what I can wrap my mind around. If you are living in your, "I can't believe this is real," then you are in your latter days. If you must pinch yourself, you are living in your new reality. The bible tells us that the latter will be greater than the former. If I live life as though I'm in my latter (season of prosperity) I do not have to wait until I get to heaven. There is no need for latter days in heaven because every day will be a latter day on earth.

There is a fighter in you. Others may mislabel the fighter in you as arrogant, prideful or conceited. But the sooner I accepted my own determination and fortitude was not contingent upon anyone else's approval, the more confident I became. It is true that others will try to place you in a box due to their own insecurities and shortcomings. But you are not responsible for their feelings. You must be accountable to yourself and God.

One day, as I was reflecting on my life, reality hit me…I AM A SURVIVOR! I took for granted that I endured the toughest challenges anyone could have faced, yet I got through it. I survived countless situations. I would sometimes reminisce over all I have encountered, and I can truly say it has been the grace of God that carried me. No, it does not add up. I should have had at least three to four mental breakdowns. There were countless times I would cry myself to sleep as I held a teddy bear that belonged to one of my daughters. Many of those nights, I hoped that

I would not wake up at all because the pain and pressure were so great. Unbeknownst to me, I was being groomed to be a warrior. Each fight that we encounter continues to strengthen our faith and resolve. It does not matter how long an individual can claimed to have a personal relationship with The Most-High, they are not exempt from extreme trials.

It is the fighter in you that will cause you to take on challenges that others would run from. It was David's willingness to challenge the giant that soon ushered him to be king over Israel. When the warrior in you awakens, your courage awakens.

I am reminded of the movie Lion King when Simba realized he was the new king. It was not until after his revelation of himself that he began to walk as the king of the jungle. As he walked with his head held high, his confidence of what he felt on the inside demanded the respect from those on the outside.

God is waiting on you to take your place and to roar! Stop waiting on others to know your place. God is waiting on you to position yourself, then those around you can be set free and truly walk in the grace and mercy God has already paid the price for them to walk in. Get in position, discover yourself, and you will soon be discovered by others.

CHAPTER 8

LET THE WALLS FALL DOWN

After being molested at my grandmother's house, I grew numb inside. It was a shocking experience and it left me feeling confused. It is easy for victims of any kind of abuse to put walls around their hearts, especially vile acts like rape and molestation. If you are presently feeling the pain of rejection, abandonment, and victimization, know that I identify with you. It is in this deep place of numbness and pain that you must acknowledge that you need help. Your acknowledgement will start you on the journey of healing.

I kept that a secret until shortly after I graduated high school. I later found out that I was not the only person that was violated. Apparently, I did not feel comfortable telling my mother or grandmother immediately about what happened. I tried to push it to the back of my mind and forget that it occurred. Fast forward 46 years later, I discovered there is no such thing as forgetting traumatic experiences. The best thing that I could have done was to be honest with myself and tell my mother about how I was violated.

Just to reiterate, the first step to healing is first being honest with yourself and second is to admit that you need help. I know you may have been betrayed, but you still must let your walls down. When you build walls around yourself as an attempt to make sure nobody will ever get the chance to hurt you again, you also become a prisoner of hurt and bitterness. The same walls you have built are the same walls that will keep the right people out.

My dear sister and dear brother, you are hindering the help you secretly wish you had. I can assure you that you are not the first, neither will you be the last person to experience pain. You must love life more than the pain you have experienced. You cannot allow people or situations to push you to the edge of life and be willing to give up and end it all.

Newsflash—If you decide to end it all, I can assure you the people who hurt you will probably go on with their lives. They will not cry over you that long, perhaps not at all. Instead they will replace you and live life without you. Walls serve as blockers. They keep life from you and eventually suck the life out of you.

> "Now Jericho was straightly shut up because of the children of Israel; none went out, and none came in"
> —(Joshua 6:1 KJV)

We talked about God's providence of isolation but did not go deep into self-isolation. Self-isolation is harmful and can lead to social isolation. These have been linked to depression, fear, loneliness, self-hate, and self-sabotage. Walls can also hinder our ability to discern accurately. Life has seasons and so does the friendships and the relationships we encounter. We must learn to distinguish when someone has finished their assignment in our lives verses a separation devised to cause us harm. The fear of rejection will cause us to sabotage even healthy relationships. This is why emotional and mental wholeness is vital.

On my last job, I met a very nice woman. I'd been hurt and betrayed by women that I trusted as mentors, and as a result, it made me very skeptical of other women. Even though I wanted to keep the wall up and stay in that place of isolation, I allowed myself to trust. She has been not only a good friend, but the sister that I needed.

Allowing the walls to come down does not take away the pain you've suffered. Allowing the walls to come down means you no longer want to be held captive in your own prison. To be imprisoned is not just bars in a cell with a thin mattress on the floor. Imprisonment is most often in the mind.

If we are honest, a lot of pain is self-inflicted. By that I mean, governed by our choices. I thought about my children and my desires to attain my degrees. I recognized that while my plans were good, I put them on the back burner when I started dating. At the time, my emotional needs outweighed my ambitions. However, I realized that delaying my goals created more hardship and pain. The most common mistake that many people make is looking for someone else, usually the opposite sex, to bring them happiness. When there is a void of love, we tend to fill that void with people. While we long for that love our souls crave, we often overlook red flags. Women, particularly, look for security in a man. All too often, women and men end up in unhealthy marriages seeking the security that was denied to them by their parents. Their neediness causes them to stay in relationships that are often emotionally, mentally, and physically abusive. Unfortunately, some partners recognize the emotional deficiency in women and will use it to their advantage.

It often starts off good, but where two are unequally yoked, it is disaster waiting to happen! Yes, marriage is good, but not all marriages are God ordained. When you insist on doing things that you think you need in your life, you tie God's hands. Our minds cannot fathom the reality of what we really need.

Man looks at the outer appearance while God looks at the heart. Instead of looking for other people to make you feel happy, you must allow God to fill the voids in your life. When God begins to fill those voids, there is no need to seek happiness outside of Him. As you submit to this process, your focus shifts from what you think you need to trusting your Heavenly Father. Now don't get me wrong. I am not saying you do not need relationships. I am saying it is not healthy to depend on another person for your happiness. Remember, we have an adversary who seeks anyone he can defile and devour.

> "Be alert and of sober mind. Your enemy the devil prowls around like a roaring lion looking for someone to devour"
> —(1 Peter 5:8 NIV)

The institution of marriage should be entered into carefully and not haphazardly. God designed marriage to take place among two individuals who are equally yoked. When we allow God to choose our mates, it doesn't mean everything will be perfect, but he will lead us in navigating through any choppy waters.

Only He knows the man or woman who is suitable for us. However, if we insist on doing things our way, and enter into a covenant with someone that has not been ordained or approved by God, we will experience unnecessary pain. When we choose to do it our way, we are saying yes to all the hidden and deceptive things that may come out of it.

For example, I know a woman who had to choose between two men that she could marry. Both men were suitable men, but only one would be best suited for her. Fortunately, she chose and accepted God's best for her. Within the early years of their marriage, she was faced with a severe health crisis that should have ended in death. Because God's plan for her did not include her being defeated by illness, her life has been spared. Her husband stood by her side throughout the entire ordeal. If she would have chosen less than God's best, she might have endured her trials alone.

Another example is a woman I knew who chose to marry without seeking God. And because of it, she encountered many painful things, including a health crisis. I AM THAT WOMAN! I faced cancer alone and went through a painful divorce at the same time. However, I am convinced that cancer is not of God and neither is divorce.

When facing challenges alone, one cannot help but wonder and ask God why? Marriages end for a variety of reasons, and we may never know all the answers, but I have learned, that choosing a mate that isn't a part of God's perfect plan isn't wise. That person hasn't been graced to walk alongside you. If God says no to a person, that does not mean that person is a bad person. It means He cares so much for you that He does not want to see you go through pain that can be avoided. Also, the no could simply mean not right now. When a person isn't "graced" to walk with you, it is easy to disregard their marriage vows, especially when difficult times arise.

Again, the self-inflicted pain implies that the pain could have been avoided. I am sure most people have heard the saying "You made your bed, now you must lay in it." Most of the time we ignore the advice or wisdom that comes from those who can clearly see the direction we are headed in. Ignoring wise counsel leads to unfavorable outcomes.

Understand that no one is exempt from challenges and even great marriages will have their share. The difference is in how one chooses to handle those pitfalls. It is much easier to walk through the valley with someone fighting for you instead of against you.

There are similarities that exist among earthly parents and God. When walking in obedience unto God and we find ourselves in a place that was not planned, the consequences are not as severe compared to an individual that blatantly chooses to continue to operate in disobedience. When we choose to ignore the warnings, the consequences from God are reflective of such.

Oftentimes, when my children try their best to comply with my wishes and they fall short of doing so, I am more lenient in the consequences. Whereas, if they refused to follow instructions that are given to them repeatedly, I will not be lenient in the punishment. God is no different. That explains why some people who have made bad decisions and continue to make bad decisions, continue to have constant turmoil. God is not merciful when you insist on doing it your way. He will sit back and let you think that your way of doing things are profitable for you, only to find it takes way too much work to maintain those things that we started.

Surrender to God. His way yields promising results without all the "extras" to maintain what has already started. Free your mind and allow God to figure it out!

CHAPTER 9

YOU vs THEM

The famous cliché… "The apple does not fall far from the tree," can have many truths to it; however, it does not have to apply to your life. Regardless, if you have accepted Jesus as your Savior or not, you do not have to be the product of your family tree.

As a little girl, I remember waking up on Sunday mornings, dressing myself and walking to church alone. At the time, I did not fully understand what was going on, other than I had a desire to go to church.

I thought it was strange, after all, the other youths that were present were there with their parents. There were a few times that my aunt would take me to church with her. Those were the typical holidays that everyone else attended.

Although my family did not attend church regularly, God was increasing my desire for Him. He is not limited in the actions of others. Regardless of the lack of spiritual guidance, He still chose me and began to manifest His works in me.

I read the book of Revelation and not knowing how to interpret it, caused me to fear. I asked my grandmother for clarity on the things I read, and she was not equipped to help me understand the Word. For the record, I am not bashing my family; I want to magnify the fact that you do not have to be the product of your family tree. I also understand that everyone including some scholars differ in their interpretations of scripture. One can't gain deep understanding without the aid of the Holy Spirit. The Bible says that He (The Holy Spirit) leads us into all truth. The baptism of the Holy Spirit was also lacking in my family. Again, this is to show you, that many are going to be "first" in their family. God always chooses a vessel to call forward. Being called out and set apart is also to help break generational cycles and curses off the bloodline. Additionally, God will use you to help encourage others who have walked similar paths such as yourself. Your family tree does not define, dictate or give direction for your life. You can decide or shall I say, you can cooperate and participate with God's plan for your life. With God alone, there is assurance that He does not need a cosigner with your past or where you have come from.

 The tug on my life by God became stronger over the years. I had a heart to please God. Nevertheless, the one issue that I struggled with from time to time was premarital sex. My issue was not visible as a smoker or drinker, but it carried the same weight. During those moments of sin, I was looking for the affection and affirmation that I never received from my earthly father. I longed for the love that I should have received from him.

 As a result, I began to seek out a false image of love and affirmation from men. I engaged in the act of premarital sex, but I could not enjoy it because it seemed like I could feel God's eyes on me. Many times, I could not look at myself in the mirror afterwards. I felt dirty. I identified with Adam and Eve in the garden when God asked what they had done.

> *"When the woman saw that the fruit of the tree was good for food and pleasing to the eye, and also desirable for gaining wisdom, she took some and ate it. She also gave some to her husband, who was with her, and he ate it. Then the eyes of both of them were opened, and they realized they were naked; so they sewed fig leaves together and made coverings for themselves. Then the man and his wife heard the sound of the Lord God as he was walking in the garden in the cool of the day, and they hid from the Lord God among the trees of the garden. But the Lord God called to the man, "Where are you?" He answered, "I heard you in the garden, and I was afraid because I was naked; so I hid." And he said, "Who told you that you were naked? Have you eaten from the tree that I commanded you not to eat from?"* (Genesis 3:6-11 NIV).

I made a commitment to God that I would save sex for marriage. After I made my commitment to God, I shared my commitment with the guy I was dating at the time, and he absolutely blew it. He even went to my grandmother and aunt to discuss such foolery (so he thought) and they immediately sided with him.

Since I was already having sex and I was no longer a virgin, they said I could never return to such an innocent state, and it made no sense to take such a stand. Besides that, no man would ever want me if I refuse to have sex with him. Those were just a few of the comments I had to endure as they gave their speeches against abstinence. We debated back and forth, but refuting was to no avail. They stood their ground. They didn't understand the spiritual consequences of disobeying God. I stood on the Word of God and my commitment, but eventually fell into sin again.

The verbal abuse at home often pushed me into the arms of my boyfriend for comfort. Seeking solace at his house was my way of escape. But, instead of fleeing to my then boyfriend's house, I should have sought a better solution, such as a counselor. As bad as I wanted relief from the abuse, I made the mistake of thinking a man could give me what I was looking for.

Not only was it far from being the truth, but I perpetuated the lie by thinking that was my only way out. In my search for acceptance, I found more of the thing that I was running from—abuse. The arms I ran to only enjoyed the benefit of sex. It seemed as a win-win situation for him. I do not blame him for enjoying sex, it wasn't his fault that I thought I could cover the pain.

Because of the hurt I had on the inside, I willingly agreed to use sex as a band-aid. As a result, I got pregnant. Contrarily, the very ones who mocked my decision to be abstinent and encouraged me to have sex, strongly opposed my decision to keep my baby. I strongly believe my grandmother allowed the enemy to deceive her by trying to coerce me into an action of murder against my unborn son. If I was going to have an abortion, it was going to be my decision alone.

I had good intentions of not having premarital sex, however, I still committed sin. The act of premarital sex caused pain that God never intended for me to experience. I can say that my son is doing well now. He is a college graduate. I have absolutely no regrets for the decision to keep him; he changed my life for the better.

Although I am a single parent and have been for most of my children's lives, God never changed His mind or His pursuit of me. While it is common and natural for the family to want the younger family members to follow in their footsteps, that was not God's plan for my life. You may be thinking that is absurd. Why would anyone want the same thing for a younger family member? It happens all the time.

I will give another example. There are many married women who truly believe God hates divorce. Since God hates divorce many believe they must endure abuse, cheating, and toxic relationships. As a result, those married women who have been unhappy for years hide behind the mask of religion. Deep inside of their minds, they believe God wants them to remain in that situation. Unfortunately, these same married women will encourage younger married women to remain and fight for their marriages.

While it is important to work on a marriage, it is not healthy to remain in a marriage that is causing emotional and physical pain. I made the mistake and remained in the marriage thinking it would get better. I thought I could pray my way through. The scriptures on adultery and marriage have been misinterpreted to mean that a woman is to stay in an abusive relationship. The misrepresentation of information that is conveyed by the women that have chosen to remain for the sake of their children or a false sense of security leads other women to continue in a vicious cycle of accepting abuse.

You do not have to be a product of your family tree. Even now, with the setbacks, you still have time to change the trajectory of your life. Make a change! Make a commitment to choose God's plan and ways for your life. The moment you accept Jesus as your Lord and Savior, you immediately are an heir of God. God said that He would make all things new and you are now a new creation in Him (2 Corinthians 5:17). Take advantage of this clean slate, an opportunity to right the wrong you have done. Embrace the newness of your new-found family, the family of God!

When seeking advice from others, there are things you must consider, such as whether the advice given is from a healthy perspective and solid biblical wisdom.

Oftentimes, when people give advice, they do so out of their own experiences. When I began to look for my dream car, I did not go alone. I took my brother from another mother with me. I thought he would make sure I would not be taken advantage of. He performed that task with flying colors. His presence and knowledge of cars were intended to ensure my car buying experience would be positive. He and I spoke about the vehicle that I wanted and the budget I was working with.

There was the implied misconception that I should have allowed him to select the car I was buying, although I was paying for the vehicle. This assumption can be compared to that of a mother and her soon to be college student. The mother may have a difficult time in allowing her son or daughter to decide on the university they desire to attend, versus mom making that decision, while refusing to relinquish her role to a certain extent.

    I was somewhat bothered by his demeanor but remembered he had already assumed the position as an older brother. While I do not believe his intentions were ill willed, I do believe he wanted me to make the wisest decision that I could live without regret. Nevertheless, I was reminded of the promise that God made to me regarding my dream vehicle. My focus had to remain on what God had already told me, while not being moved by the opinions of others. You see, a year before I actually purchased my dream car, I was told that I would be blessed with it. I did not understand how it would come to pass, considering I was a full-time student and a single mom.

    Previous experiences have taught me to trust in the promises of The Most High. Trying to figure out how it will happen is enough to cause anyone to doubt the likelihood of it coming to pass. It does not matter what your "IT" may be, it is important that you keep the faith that it will happen. Although you may not see every detail, those moments of waiting for the manifestation of it are later used as building blocks for your faith. I have personally learned to wait without panicking. This level of assurance in Him is the catalyst of my steadfast belief in Him. My reassurance from God made it possible for me to stay focused on what I wanted and not what the salesman wanted to sell me. I visited the dealership two times prior to my purchase. During the first visit, the sales agent was showing me cars that I did not want. Prior to arriving at the dealership that day, the same sales agent had 6-7 vehicles that were in my budget to choose from. I had spoken to him on the phone and but when I arrived at the dealership those vehicles were no longer available. We were back at square one.

Not only did I know the vehicle that I wanted, but I also sought God in prayer. I did not pray haphazardly, but rather, specifically and strategically. I prayed about the amount of money I was willing to pay, but I also asked God to do certain things if it was the vehicle, he wanted me to have. I did not want more or less than God's desire for me.

I wanted what God wanted for me so much, that I could smell a luxury car. I could see the luxury car at my residence. I could see myself driving this luxury car. In reality, the luxury car was already mine. I had aligned myself to the will of my Heavenly Father. I was not willing to settle for less or compromise. Through all the pain I have gone through, that year alone, God fine-tuned my ability to hear Him even more. If we would just settle ourselves, we will know without a shadow of doubt God's plans and desires for us.

It was a few minutes before closing and the salesman showed me a car that a customer dropped off for them to sell. The vehicle was parked in the garage and was not ready to be placed on the parking lot. I saw the vehicle and loved it. I could smell the new car scent.

The vehicle had 41,000 miles. I walked away from that dealership as the owner of my dream car — BMW X5 and it was LOADED!

There was a time when I was vulnerable to the thoughts and opinions of others. I would have missed this God ordained blessing, if I were still in that place. I'm grateful to God because that vulnerability has dissipated. I chose to get in God's Word and presence for myself. It is one thing to repeat what someone else says versus what you read for yourself in the Bible and the revelation God gives you.

My faith grew even more, along with my confidence in God. I watched how things progressed and manifested in the form of my dream vehicle. The acquisition of this vehicle was not predicated on what my budget would allow me to buy, nor the fact that I had a one-income producing household. I learned from that moment it was not my job to figure out the how and the when, instead, it was my job to believe. With the increase of faith, also came a bold conviction of the things God wanted for me, despite the limits society often tried to place on me. I've also learned that people who operate out of jealousy, will believe God for themselves and view your circumstances as conditional for God's blessings. The truth of the matter is they really do not want to see you progress.

I remember being told by my sister that God may want to bless me with a car, but a BMW was not part of His plan for me. Instead, she shared the type of vehicle in which she thought was more suitable for me, based on the fact that I was a single mom of five children.

My oldest child was out of the home, attending college. Therefore, the vehicle was the perfect size for my family. It is common for others to have the faith to believe The Most-High for their wants and needs, while limiting that same God regarding the needs of others. My sister could not accept the idea of how God wanted to bless me, regardless of my circumstances. Again, this can be compared to a family being blessed with an apartment versus a home. Both are blessings but the preference would be homeownership. She may have meant well, but she placed limits on God based on my status.

It's amazing at how those same people can believe God for themselves and have no faith for others. People do not have the same faith level as you; therefore, they cannot comprehend the idea of a once vulnerable individual progressing to hearing the voice of God for his or herself. I had become so desperate for God and all He wanted for me that I began to seek Him until I knew without doubt that was His will concerning me.

Many people miss opportunities of blessings or a move of God based on ideologies of other people. What God has for me is not based on what someone else believes I am entitled to have. What God has for you is not based on what I think you should have. What God has for you is not based on what you think you should have. Instead, it is based on the sovereign will of God.

I had to learn to love people from afar and not receive their lack of faith for my situation. The assistance of other people is not necessary for you to believe God to do the impossible in your life.

> He replied, "Because you have so little faith. Truly I tell you, if you have faith as small as a mustard seed, you can say to this mountain, 'Move from here to there,' and it will move. Nothing will be impossible for you"
> —(Matthew 17:20 NIV)

When given the diagnosis of cancer, I cried some and then I stopped. I controlled the voices that were around me. I did not seek others' opinions on what they thought my plan of action should be. Instead, I sought God for His plan of action. I immediately began to say everything God said about the cancer in my body. It was during this time in which I had to go back to the word of The Most-High regarding healing. Just as I had to trust in what He promised me regarding my dream vehicle, I had to trust the same God concerning my health. The subject matter may change, but principles never change.

I did not allow my mind to wander in the direction of death. I began to take control of my environment. I distanced myself from every negative thought. If it was going to take positive energy from me, I got rid of it. During that process, I learned that the changes made had to be lifelong changes and not quick-fix changes based on a temporary circumstance.

You must decide how close you want negative energy to be near you. While you cannot control the thoughts of other people, you can change the proximity of the enemy you choose to allow in your immediate space. As for me,

I could not afford the negative energies of others to be near me.

Whether we know it or not, the thoughts and feelings of others can be projected on to us. Basically, you do not want to feed off another person's fears. Fear is based on false evidence. We must believe that God delights in blessings us.

CHAPTER 10

YOUR LIFE, YOUR DREAMS, YOUR WAY

Some dreams are too big to hold, and you may be eager to share them but that is not always wise. The truth is not everyone will be excited for the dreams God has placed within you. Some are on assignment from the enemy to get you to give up. These people are known as Dream Killers. There is no way to distinguish them by looks, pedigree, anointing or social status. Some even exist in your interpersonal relationships.

The purpose of the dream killer is to stifle you from germinating the seed of the dreams embedded on the inside of you. Dream killers can also be those who are afraid to move forward in their own lives and in essence, will project that same inhibition onto you. You can identify them by their reactions to other people's dreams and listening to their conversation. You will hear the negativity and toxicity in their voices and observe their demeanor. When you identify them, keep them at bay but do not develop hate or bitterness toward them. In fact, you can learn from them. I know that sounds crazy! But you can learn what not to do. Another key thing you can take away from someone who tries to kill your vision is persistence. There is something about determined faith that births things into existence. Unfortunately, if we are not careful, dream killing can become contagious. Therefore, you must learn to encourage rather than discourage the dreams of others.

Remember dreams are only the beginning phase of vision. Eventually, you will have to outline or detail the strategic plans for bringing your vision to fruition. Your dreams must be the priority. Keep your focus and embrace the methodical steps that God has given you. Even if it has never been done that way before, you must remain true to your own vision.

> **"What good is it, my brothers and sisters, if someone claims to have faith but has no deeds? Can such faith save them?"**
> **—(James 2:14 NIV)**

True visionaries do not wake up one day and decide to do something because everyone else is doing it. They have a clear picture and a clear purpose. Knowing exactly where you want to go and how you will achieve it, will drive your passion.

In order to see your vision manifest in unprecedented ways, you must never stop learning or developing your gifts. Visionaries are key to any business and/or ministry. The ability of a visionary to broaden and expand what currently exist will not only produce great profitability, but sustainability as well. They can literally make something out of what others deem as "nothing."

Not only do visionaries see beyond what is present, they also know precisely the time for execution. It isn't perfect conditions that will birth vision, but the right posture that will birth potential. God reveals the hidden potential within each of us, as we step forward in obedience to His will. Controlling our mental state by visualizing what we want, verses where we are will keep us focused forward. I used the technique of controlling my mental state during some of the most difficult times in my life. By focusing on something positive, I was able to walk through everything in faith. It is important to maintain a proper mental life.

Your mental life is your ram in the bush and reminder of God's purpose and plan for your life. As a dreamer myself, I must admit keeping my mental life fortified with positive affirmations, enabled me to keep going, when I wanted to quit.

During the time of my radiation treatments, I was very limited in using my voice. There were times just drinking sips of water produced excruciating pain. I'd make a fist to help me stay strong as I swallowed. That was my reality, however, in my mental life I would close my eyes and dream that I was talking to millions of people without strain, and independently of man's assisted devices, yet dependent on my Heavenly Father.

My mental life has sustained and continues to sustain me. This can also be equated to speaking to a group of people and finding that focal point in the room. If a focal point is not found, it is easy to succumb to the faces of the people in the crowd and allow fear to get you off focus.

As a cancer survivor and a survivor of life statistically, I have discovered that healing comes in different forms. Without focusing on the Word of God, and maintaining my prayer life, I can assure you, I would have lost my mind. I know for sure I would not have overcome all of the obstacles that were designed to destroy me. I thank God for giving me just a glimpse of what He had in store for me. The greatest joy of being a dreamer is that you do not have all the steps in the beginning. God can and often gives us a portion or a glimpse so that we can hold on and develop confidence in Him. He who began a good work in you, shall bring it to completion. I dare you to step out on the ledge of life and dare to be a dreamer.

> 'And Jesus said unto them, "Because of your unbelief: for verily I say unto you, if ye have faith as a grain of mustard seed, ye shall say unto this mountain, Remove hence to yonder place; and it shall remove; and nothing shall be impossible unto you'"
> —(Matthew 17:20 KJV)

Speak to the reality of your today and watch God align your reality life to your mental life. Dream big! The same faith that is required to believe God for meeting your everyday needs is the same faith required to believe God for your mental life dreams.

A dear woman once told me, "Sarah, God is in heaven with a $1000 bill asking for change. He is asking for change because we tend to ask for only a $100, when He desires to give us so much more."

Dare to believe that God has $1000 in His hand and desires to give it ALL to you, IF only you would believe.

We are not our past, but our past makes us who we are. The fact that you made it through, when you could have given up, highlights the fighter in you. You had a lot of drag out fights. Yes, the enemy took low blows to your self-esteem, but you continued to get back up.

The enemy of our souls does not fight fair. He fights those that are a direct threat to his kingdom of darkness. But true fighters continue to get back up. Fighters are not punks. The fight alone does not define you, but the fact that you got back up is what defines you. All that you have been through…THIS IS WHO YOU ARE. You are the "get back up woman" who refuses to die, regardless of the bad report from the doctor. You are the "get back up man" who refuses to settle for mediocrity. Make no apologies for getting back up after every fight. The fights you endured were necessary tools to help shape who you are today. Each fight was instrumental in the development of your strength and character.

Can you honestly say that you would be where you are today if it were not for the obstacles? Every fight you fought was a fixed fight. A fight to get you closer to your destiny. That is what the fight was all about…you fulfilling God's destiny for your life. God has a greater purpose for you! When God created you, He had more in mind. As much as you may love or not love your job, God called you to do more than go to work, get a check and pay bills. God created you to be a world changer, a game changer. That is right… a game changer! Game changers are leaders. True leaders lead by example. Whether you know it or not, there are people, friends, coworkers, family members that are watching you to see how you are going to handle this fight you are in right now. The devil may hit you real hard, but don't give in. Make the enemy of your soul mad by making him hit you harder. The enemy of your soul is beyond angry with you because you will not give up. Every attack you have faced signifies the temper tantrums the devil is having right now because you will not give up. Refuse to give in to the enemy.

No matter how hard you fought, there was some good that came out of it. It may not have been your fault, yet there was something you learned from it. No, you were not the initiator, but you gained something from that situation that has helped you to endure subsequent challenges. Let's face it, no professional boxer gets in the ring to fight an opponent that they have never prepared themselves to fight. The boxer had the opportunity to know their opponent in advance. You and I, unfortunately, do not get that opportunity to know the fights that will soon become our reality.

Since our God is such a loving God, each fight He allows into our life will build on the next fight which is usually more intense than the previous fight. The fight is for our own perfecting. The sooner we understand that the fight is fixed, the sooner we will grasp the revelation that it is not the character of God to allow us to go through things that will destroy us. Everything that happens to us is God allowed. The good, bad and ugly are all allowed by God. I refuse to give the devil that kind of credit that implies that the devil is in control and God has no say so in the matters of our lives. I choose to believe the devil has to get permission from God before he launches an attack against us.

> "The Lord said to Satan, 'Have you considered my servant Job?' There is no one on earth like him; he is blameless and upright, a man who fears God and shun evil.'
> 'Does Job fear God for nothing?' Satan replied. Have you not put a hedge around him and his household and everything he has? You have blessed the works of his hands, so that his flocks and herds are spread throughout the land.
> But now stretch out your hand and strike everything he has, and he will surely curse you to your face.' The Lord said to Satan, 'Very well, then, everything he has is in your power, but on the man himself do not lay a finger.' Then Satan went out from the presence of the Lord" (Job 1:8-12 NIV).

Statistics...Statistics...Statistics... are all about numbers. In my opinion, statistics are specifically for those individuals that rely heavily on the data that has not been proven to be tested time and time again. In the realm of science, no good scientist formulates a hypothesis without the hypothesis being tested repeatedly. Statistics and science are counter relative. Statistics formulate a general hypothesis without the proven repetition of the proposed data. Statistics are fortified upon part of the truth and not the whole truth. According to statistics, most single-family homes set the perpetual negative dominoe effect in the lives of the children. It is often said that the children that are a product of single-family homes are less likely to succeed and less likely to break the status quo. The questions that I like to ask the person or persons that are responsible for collecting such data is who are the subjects and where did you find them?

While there may be some truth to the hypothesis, it is not the complete truth. You see "some truth" and "the truth" are not created equal. Let's take a look at another example. 2+2=4, 3+1=4, 4+0=4. As you have witnessed, there are more than a few ways to find the sum of 4. However, the examples given are not the only examples of the sum of 4. You have (-14)+18=4 and 3 ¼ + ¾ = 4.

The problem I have with statistics is that presumed numbers are based on limited information. As you can see, the truth you decide to embrace is solely predicated on either some truth or "the truth."

It is very imperative that you take away from the above examples that you have the power to dictate how the story of your life will play out. The ability to be statistically correct or scientifically proven time and time again, lies within you. Statistically, women usually cannot conceive children in old age. We do hear of some women in their 70's having babies, but this is not the norm. And never in their 90's. However, let's look at the Biblical example of Sarah, Abraham's wife. Scientifically, God had a greater purpose and plan for Sarah's life. God, being infinite, operated outside of the laws of statistics and science and touched Sarah's womb for her to conceive a child.

> "Now the Lord was gracious to Sarah as he had said, and the Lord did for Sarah what he had promised. Sarah became pregnant and bore a son to Abraham in his old age, at the very time God had promised him. Abraham gave the name Isaac to the son Sarah bore him. When his son Isaac was eight days old, Abraham circumcised him, as God commanded him. Abraham was a hundred years old when his son Isaac was born to him Sarah said, "God has brought me laughter, and everyone who hears about this will Laugh with me." And she added, "Who would have said to Abraham that Sarah would Nurse children? Yet, I have borne him a son in his old age.…" (Genesis 21:1-7 NIV).

What God did for Abraham and Sarah cannot be confined to science or statistics. The things you are going through at this very moment cannot be confined to the limited data that someone has. Do not allow an individual to mark you for doom based on your situation. May I suggest you begin to seek God for your life, begin to seek God for the answers that only He can supply. God could have allowed Abraham and Sarah to conceive sooner. Why did God wait until they were old to make good on a promise? I personally believe God used Abraham and Sarah as the first example of His promise to mankind. They crossed a threshold.

CHAPTER 11

SURVIVAL OF THE THRESHOLD

Threshold. Out of all things, THRESHOLD! What is it? What does it look like? How does it happen? According to Merriam Webster a threshold is an end or boundary. It represents the place or point of entering or beginning. Some of the synonyms for threshold are, brink, cusp, edge, point, and verge.

On one side of the threshold are the reminders of what you had to overcome. On the other side of the threshold are all the effects of how you got there. Each side of a threshold has two different perspectives. Examples of thresholds happen when a first-time college student from his or her family finally graduates from college, or it could be a single parent who finally gave up after trying to overcome obstacles that other family members also faced. In order to move forward, one step would not be enough. As one foot is placed in front to take a step forward, the other foot is left in limbo (a nonfunctional place).

You cannot perform basic functions, such as sneezing, while in a place of limbo, without falling.

As you began walking, the foot in the back is in limbo, sneezing will cause you to lose your balance. This denotes a place or position of inactivity.

To live life in a state of limbo is equivalent to being stagnated. Doing too much of one thing can be dangerous.

The area that is left untouched by your existence suffers tremendously. To be in a nonfunctional place does not mean there is no activity. As mentioned, you cannot sneeze without falling in this place. Yet, you can move your eyes and sustain yourself without falling. The words "functioning" and "activity" do not hold the same meaning and should not be used interchangeably.

In order to move forward, an additional step is required, this is what we call the "second step." The longer it takes to move the other foot, the longer you will remain in limbo.

What steps must you take to cross the thresholds in your life? The step you must take is determined by the distance between both steps. Follow me if you will, let's go back to the childhood game, "Green Light, Red Light." The kid closest to the person leading the game must make their last stride big enough to actually touch the leader in order to win. Smaller strides delayed the other kids from winning. Therefore, in playing this game, it's all about the length of the strides. The strides taken determine how long it would take for someone to win. While playing this game as a child, there were loose dogs roaming the neighborhood.

If you were anything like my aunt, who was terrified of dogs, you would forfeit your place of sure victory based on the fear of dogs. It did not matter if the dog had no teeth, my aunt was going to run. Some dogs are literally all bark and no bite. In fact, I've seen dogs who would not chase after a flying stick, but if they see you run… you can count on them running after you. Remaining in position and determining not to react to the presence of the dog would cause the animal to stop trying to chase you and move out of your way. It is best to stand still, continue your strides, and be the winner of "Green Light, Red Light."

I would be remiss if I did not show you how to apply surviving the thresholds of your life. Allow me to reminisce back three years ago, I thought I was finished with the writing for this book. I was excited and told everyone I met about my first soon-to-be published book. I reached out to publishers, but to no avail. I researched the pros and cons of self-publishing versus hiring a publishing company. I thought I was complete, but there was more to add to the book you are now reading. Many days I pondered if I should really add more to the book? Thus, I delayed. I found myself struggling. Having one foot forward, I had the activity of eye movement, yet I was limited in functioning properly. I was stuck in that place of limbo. Mentally, I could see what needed to happen but did not seem to know how to take the next step.

As a single mom of four daughters living at home, I was constantly faced with the feelings of being overwhelmed with the demands of motherhood pulling at me, the demands of being a graduate student and trying my best to maintain a personal life. I desperately wanted things to balance out, but there were simply not enough hours in a day to meet those demands. Fearful of not publishing my first book, all while feeling mentally and physically fatigued, I began to pray to God to allow me to rest. I specifically asked for rest that did not include me being sick or being admitted into the hospital. God later revealed to me that I would be fired from my job and I could not prevent it. About two or three months later, it happened, and I was fired from my job. While I was forewarned, I was also shocked that it would happen just before the holidays. Even with the set-back, I was able to buy new tires, purchase a new refrigerator and replace my washer, all while unemployed, simply because I was willing to take a second step. That second step sealed the deal and showed me that God had a far greater plan for me.

Afraid of the unknown, I was unsure of how everything would come together. I began to look within myself for behaviors that contradicted my purpose. Those behaviors included fear, procrastination, feelings of being stuck, feelings of being overwhelmed, and the fear of others not wanting to hear what I had to say. The greatest fear of all was my ability to speak and to be understood.

The time that lapsed from the initial step to the next step became the place of stagnation for me. I was afraid of falling back into the same spot that I was in before.

Not only are those feelings a contradiction of where you are going, but those feelings are natural feelings during the crossing of the threshold. In fact, those feelings serve as a compass and the proximity of your "soon to cross over" threshold experience.

As you can see, the threshold is the most critical moment. Timing is everything. Strategic movements are vital. If there is a lack of timing and lack of strategic movement, you run the risk of sabotaging all the steps you've made. It is very crucial that you remind yourself of all the small steps you've made. In doing so, you maintain the momentum of victory. In maintaining the momentum long enough to reach the threshold, the journey will be met with a different level of challenges. However, as you focus on your "step two" you will soon discover the reasons for the increased challenges you faced. A common mistake that individuals make is to think once they have a taste of victory, they are exempt from the feelings of defeat, despair and fear. Each life experience prepares and strengthens us for the next season of our lives. It has the effect of a trampoline with the ability to thrust us into complete victory. The thrust provides an advantage we could have only experienced by not quitting. The fight on the inside of you that will not allow you to quit is the very character trait that qualifies you as a survivor. This is what gives you the ability to survive the threshold.

Let us look at the story of David. His life shows how he developed his momentum as he reached a threshold that led to multiple victories. As we discussed in chapter 4, David's previous victories prepared him to survive the ultimate things that were meant to defeat him. The giant was confident in his ability to annihilate young David because of his stature. Although young, David was strategic in the size of the stone that he chose to destroy Goliath. He also knew exactly where to hit Goliath with the three stones.

> *"And when the Philistine looked about, and saw David, he disdained him: for he was but a youth and a ruddy, and of a fair countenance. And the Philistine said unto David, Am I a dog, that thou comest to me with staves? And the Philistine cursed David by his*

gods. And the Philistine said to David, Come to me and I will give thy flesh unto the fowls of the air, and to the beasts of the field. Then said David to the Philistine, Thou comest to me with a sword, and with a spear, and with a shield: but I come to thee in the name of the Lord of hosts, the God of the armies of Israel, whom thou has defied. This day will the Lord deliver thee into mine hand; and I will smith thee, and take thine head from thee: and I will give the carcases of the host of the Philistines this day unto the fowls of the air, and to the wild beasts of the earth; that all the earth may know that there is a God in Israel. And all this assembly shall know that the Lord saveth not with sword and spear: for the battle is the Lord's and he will give you into our hands. And when it came to pass, when the Philistine arose, and came and drew nigh to meet David, that David hasted, and ran toward the army to meet the Philistine. And David put his hand in his bag; and took thence a stone, and slang it, and smote the Philistine in his forehead, that the stone sunk into his forehead; and he fell upon his face to the earth. So David prevailed over the Philistine with a sling and with a stone, and smote the Philistine, and slew him; but there was no sword in the hand of David" (1 Samuel 17:42-50 KJV).

The story of David is a reminder for you and I of how important it is that we face each challenge with an expectation of coming out victoriously. As it was with David, even the challenges that intimidate us will propel us into the greatest set up for victory. You and I cannot avoid those challenges. When we attempt to skip that part of the process in our lives, we hinder our ability to properly prepare for the next challenge.

CHAPTER 12

RUNNING OUT OF GAS

It is possible for survivors to literally run out of gas. By now, this book should have been in the hands of millions of readers. Instead, a series of events nearly knocked the wind out of me and prolonged the launch of my book. So, let's fast forward. I graduated with my first masters on December 7, 2018. In fact, at that moment, I asked God why didn't He allow me to die in 2014? You see, I have been through so many trials and disappointments, and I really didn't think things could get worse.

Of course, there were many victories, and I am reminded of every statistic and cycle that I've been blessed to break over my life and family, yet I felt as though I'd run out of gas. I felt that I'd come to the end of my strength. This is a place where even prayer became a struggle.

My nights became unusually long. I'd lay in bed reflecting on my life. I'd overcome many things and during my reflection, it took me back to the time where I felt as if I could not take another step. It seemed every plan I tried to formulate for myself failed and everything that could go wrong, did.

It appeared to be the worse place on the planet. I had little to no money and no child support. Every bill imaginable needed to be paid and I could not see my way out.

It was a tough season, but in that hard place, I also saw the hand of God move mightily on our behalf. I remember when my oldest daughter was graduating from high school, and I battled the emotions of being overjoyed and worried at the same time. With no money and very little gas in the car, I wasn't sure if we'd make the graduation without running out of gas. By faith, I loaded my four children into the car, fully aware I did not have enough gas to make it to the baccalaureate and back home. Within 15-20 minutes of us leaving home, the gas light came on. Totally embarrassed, yet determined that nothing would stop me, I called a friend to meet me at the gas station so that I could get some assistance. Thankfully the friend provided $45 for gas, and we were able to make it!

Thoughts were racing through my mind, and I was reminded of my biggest prayer as a mother. I prayed, "Lord, help my children to always maintain hope and never lose faith." I pray that my examples of always trusting God in difficult times will be an added anchor for them.

I also wanted to take my daughter to dinner after the ceremony, but thoughts of my failures plagued my mind. Silently I wondered, "What have I done to be in this place?" I'd submitted my life to God and relinquished my right to do what I wanted, therefore, I could not understand why this was happening? Nevertheless, we were able to go out to dinner, and to my surprise, it cost me absolutely nothing! God allowed someone to treat my daughters and I to dinner. In that place of "running out of gas," God revealed that He never left me.

It wasn't easy, but I found the mental strength needed to remind myself that my latter days would be greater than my former days. I knew if my time on earth was up, then 2014 would have been the perfect time for God to make that a reality. Cancer could have taken my life. In fact, it was in that place the curtains of my life were pulled back for all to see. Up until that point, it was my strength that pressed through each obstacle and set back, finally, I felt completely stripped. I was at the sheer mercy of God. Fully dependent upon Him for every breath. God was controlling my steps much like a puppet. He pulled the strings and directed my actions.

I'd surrendered everything I thought I wanted unto Him. I eventually realized that place of running out of gas (physical and mental strength) proved to be a divine place. It was the place where God's all sufficient grace came in.

Many make the mistake of blaming the enemy for every delay and failed plan when in fact the devil had nothing to do with it. God will allow things to happen as a reminder to us that He is committed to what He has planned for our lives. He will use our situation as an example to elevate us or "show off" just how incredible He is in our lives.

I'm sure some of you can relate to that one aunt who was known for "showing off" her kids at all the family gatherings. It did not matter that her daughter had not graduated from college, she was determined to let everyone know how smart her baby was. God is no different. He knows you are a work in progress, but you have come a long way. He is excited for the growth that has taken place in your life. What sense would it make for you and me to not have a progressive journey? As it was in my life, those hard moments in your life will serve as reminders that God is always with you and He will fulfill the promises He has made.

In fact, as I sat in bed adding more to this book, I was reminded of the importance of repeating what God said about my situation. As we run out of gas, we are forced to rely on His provision. It also signifies that we have come to an end of ourselves, which is the perfect opportunity for Him to demonstrate His strength, power and provision. As emotions tried to overtake my belief in knowing God would not withhold no good thing from me, I was determined to continue to believe all things and hope all things. It is always easier to hope for the best when things are going the way you planned. When things do not, those are the times you must remain diligent, focused, and persistent. In this moment of running out of gas, it is imperative that you reference the previous times that you had to totally depend upon God. Each reference that you and I have of God meeting us where we were, is designed to prepare us for the next chapter of our lives. Each moment of being physically, mentally and spiritually tired will always propel you and I into that next chapter of our lives.

Let's take a look at God's chosen people, the Israelites, they wondered in the wilderness for 40 years. They faced many threats from the reigning king during that time. They were in an unfamiliar territory, but God continued to remain the same. They had trust issues. They murmured and complained. They appeared to be in a place of desolation. Little did they know they were embarking upon the greatest breakthrough of their lives. They were on the verge of entering the promise land. Before they entered, everything around them seemed to contradict the promise of a "land flowing with milk and honey."

> *"And Joshua said unto the children of Israel, Come hither, and hear the words of the Lord your God. And Joshua said, Hereby ye shall know that the living God is among you, and that he will without fail drive out from before you the Canaanites, and the Hittites, and the Hivites, and the Perizzites, and the Girgashites, and the Amorites, and the Jebusites. Behold, the ark of the covenant of the Lord of all the earth passeth over before you into Jordan. And the priests that bare the ark of the covenant of the Lord stood firm on dry ground in the midst of Jordan and all the Israelites passed over on dry ground, until all the people were passed clean over Jordan"* (Joshua 3:9-11;17 KJV).

I challenge you not to look at your desolate situation, you know the situation that looks like you are literally going to die right there in that place. I challenge you to rehearse the last battle you endured that ended in victory. You see, it is the devil's job to send a slew of distractions your way in an attempt to convince you not to believe in the visions God gave you. Surely, you don't believe the devil gave you the visions you continue to have of yourself drug free, financially independent, self-sufficient and productive in your efforts to provide for your family?

Those dreams and visions are inspired by God to give you hope, and to encourage you that your season of drought or lack shall not continue forever.

I wanted to transparently share my experiences and life's lessons so that you would know that God is who He says He is. During the writing of this book, four of my five children were living in my home with me. It had been months since receiving child support. I had no income, yet my children and I still had a roof over our heads. We still had our trials. The water was disconnected twice. I could not sleep at night because of the fear of not knowing when or how things would change for me. Also, during that season, my oldest daughter's college classes were about to start. I didn't know how, but strongly believed it would all work together for our good. She had a balance of roughly $9,000 and I did not have the means to pay it. I had absolutely no idea how rent would be paid for the month either, but I was confident that I did not get this far in life on a whim of luck. I am positive that I should have had several mental breakdowns over the course of my life and know without a doubt that it was no more than God's hand upon my life. Despite what your spiritual beliefs may be, you too have gotten this far because of the protection, guidance and direction of God. God continues to show Himself strong on behalf of His people.

As a woman, I am confident that God never intended for me or any other woman to endure this level of hardship, difficulty, or stress. This is not an attempt to bash men or to make anyone look bad. I acknowledge this as my truth, and it is imperative that I portray a vivid picture of my desolate situations. It is also critical that those desolate situations reflect the strength and provision of God.

If you and I are going to be and do all that we have been purposed to do and be, it will require us to move beyond what we see. It will require us to keep moving despite what is thrown at us, despite who left, and despite who wanted to see us fold over and die. The greatest asset of a survivor is the ability to overcome any adversity that comes their way. Survivors don't just survive one battle, survivors possess quality traits that propel them to survive, thrive, and overcome each challenge. Although challenges may change, the principles remain the same. Survivors survive, thrive, and overcome.

You see, I am determined not to concern myself with how God will provide for me. One thing I know for sure, I have already endured the hardest part of my life. Those obstacles are gone. It is so easy for us to think that the challenges we face are the worst we have ever witnessed. The truth is, that last situation almost took you out, but it passed, and you are still alive to share it with others. Be encouraged. Reach back as often as you need to remind yourself that you are stronger than you know, and you are built for this.

CHAPTER 13

―――――∞―――――

FREE YOURSELF, FORGIVE YOURSELF

Many can admit when they heard the word "forgiveness" instantly they believed and were taught to forgive and forget the person(s) that offended or hurt them. Rarely is the focus centered on the importance of self-forgiveness. I can attest one hundred thousand is the number of times I hesitated to look at myself in the mirror.

Self-forgiveness is not a pass for you and I to negate our part in hurting others. Instead, it is an opportunity for us to release ourselves from the mental and emotional prisons we've created for ourselves. While you may have played an integral part, no one walks into a relationship of any kind with the intent of it being severed or strained. Understand, also that self-forgiveness may look different for everyone.

The biggest and most embarrassing thing I have had to forgive myself for was having five children and three "baby daddies" along with three failed marriages. I married three times [twice to the same man].

That part of who I am has not and is not easily embraced by others. People are critical and judgmental. People have labeled me and formed opinions of me that were centered around the outcome of those severed relationships. Very few individuals lack the maturity and wisdom to separate the actions from the actor. I've even been labeled and judged based on the actions of others towards me. I wonder, if people really think I woke up one day and decided I wanted five kids that would involve three different fathers and three failed marriages? Absolutely not! I simply made bad choices because I was wounded and lacked proper guidance.

We know generational cycles are real. And if I must be honest, my aunts dated married men, and several of the ones married had affairs. Based on the examples before me, you'd think these things were acceptable. Children were also born from these affairs. The women I grew up around did not choose men who cared about them and strived to be the best fathers they could be for their children.

Even the men in my family failed to set the proper examples of properly stewarding their children. Little did I know, I was doomed to repeat some of what I witnessed, and at that time in my life, all of it seemed normal.

When I met men who were loving, kind, and fully committed to their position as fathers and husbands, I decided that I wanted more than I experienced and was exposed to.

In fact, throughout my entire childhood and young adulthood, the one thing that resonated with me the most is that I never accepted what was around me as "MY" life. I saw it around me, but I wanted more. I may not have known what "more" looked like, but I had more than enough examples of what I knew I did not want. My wanting more did not exempt me from making poor decisions nor from reaping the consequences of them.

Eventually, the reality of my decisions began to settle, and I did not like the outcome.

I would attend a few family functions, only to have comments made about my singleness and to be asked, "Where's your man? Do you have a boyfriend?" etc. Those questions and comments can weigh on a person after a while. Eventually you will begin to adopt the attitude that something must be wrong with you if you are single. And the rush to be in a committed relationship will take precedence over wisdom and patiently waiting on God.

I had my son, who was conceived out of wedlock but lacked the meaningful presence from his father. Six years later, I eventually had my oldest daughter. The saga of life choices seemed to plague me. On the inside, I wanted to crawl under a rock and stay there forever.

On the outside, I appeared to be okay as I attended a few of the family gatherings, but deep inside I felt as though I was only good for making babies. I know this sounds horrible, but this is how I felt. It is my truth. The ability to identify my truth soon served as a catalyst to help me forgive myself.

Singleness is frowned upon, especially when you are single with children. People can make you feel inadequate because you are not tied to a mate. I lived in the shame of my mistakes because of the constant reminders. Contrary to the way singleness is perceived by our culture, God views it as a calling. Singleness is precious to God, because it enables us to focus on Him without distractions. Although my children were conceived in and out of matrimony, I acknowledge they are incredible examples of gifts given by

God. Confessing my own mistakes, kept me from placing all the blame on the men in my life. I was forced to look in the mirror and admit that I had major contributions to what went wrong in each of those relationships. Accepting where I was and forgiving myself was important because it allowed me to release myself from the shame and guilt of bad choices. I was able to take control of my life and no longer use that part of my journey as a crutch. Life is a whole lot easier to navigate without crutches. Those hard to maneuver places that you and I have endured were never conducive for the use of crutches. Ditch the crutches and watch how much better you can maneuver, duck, dodge and block most of what comes your way.

I can recall going through the process of exhausting short-term disability and seeking long term disability from my place of employment because of the cancer diagnosis. Shortly after, I was terminated.

There were people who voiced their opinions regarding my situation. Disability was not easy for me because it went against all I had planned for my life. I did not feel disabled, but I had voice restrictions that made it difficult for me to find a job. Nevertheless, I continued to hold on to every dream and vision that would require the use of my voice and that was encouraging others on a platform bigger than I could possibly imagine.

Ditching the crutches allowed me to put things into proper perspective. Every decision that I made, yielded a learning experience for me to share with others. As I begin to view things differently, I suddenly realized God takes what the enemy meant for evil and uses it for good. You and I both know that is the part of the "okie dokie" the devil does not want us to believe.

Although, it was never my dream to become a single mother of five, I cannot begin to tell you the overflowing joy each of my children have brought to my life. I do not believe I would be as effective in sharing my story without them. Things always appear to be worse than what they really are, but the truth is the hardest trials we face can produce the most fulfilling moments.

If it were not for the difficult times back then, I would not have the tenacity to continue to move forward now. Constantly referencing all I have overcome gives me the wherewithal to keep moving. Those hard to maneuver places often remind me I can overcome whatever may be thrown my way. It is so important to be the gatekeeper of your thoughts. The lens from which you choose to view life will determine the trajectory of your life.

A few days after the biopsy of my vocal cord, I had a follow up appointment with the ear, nose, and throat doctor. I had no preparation for the prognosis I would receive. It never occurred to me I was on the verge of receiving the worst possible news of my life. As I sat in the chair, still clueless that there was a possibility of a negative report, I heard these words… "You have cancer on your right vocal cord, but we caught it in the early stages."

In that moment, I thought about everything I had heard about cancer. It was a nasty, ugly word with a death sentence. My eyes immediately began to fill with tears. While the doctor was still talking, I began to suck up the tears so I could make an informed decision regarding my health. I was given the options to have surgery, which risked the possibility of me losing the little voice I did have or radiation treatments for the duration of six weeks. Needless, to say, I opted for six weeks of radiation.

Everything I'd endured in my life literally prepared me for that moment. Every church sermon, every scripture I read regarding healing became my instant reference. Because I was determined to live for my five children, negativity was not an option. I decided to take every word God said regarding healing and apply it to my life. I was crazy enough to believe whatever was written in His book would manifest in my life.

I attended most of my radiation appointments alone. Initially, I did not think about the support I did not have present with me like the other patients had with them. But when reality of being alone hit me, I immediately had to shake off the feeling of abandonment and rejection. Again, determined to live, I researched and discovered how colors play a major role in healing and your attitude about yourself and life. Determined to live for my five children, I purposefully dressed as if I was going to attend a Mary Kay skin care class.

I was determined I was going to live and there was absolutely nothing anyone could have said to convince me otherwise. Fast forward to the end of six weeks of radiation, I had a chance to talk with the staff and my nurse at UTSW, who was beyond phenomenal.

He shared with me how they would watch me come in every day for radiation. They were in awe of my beauty and literally felt sad for me because they felt the radiation treatments were going to do harm to my body. I continued to be positive and joyful. I dressed to impress for each doctor's appointment. I was determined that my outer appearance would not reflect what I was going through. I completed six weeks of radiation, along with maintaining my gym routine five days a week at LA Fitness. My body never responded to the radiation in the manner they predicted.

My nurse told me the area in which I received the radiation treatments normally turns black. I was also told that I should have also been on a feeding tube, but I never had one. It was at that moment I knew God was very present in my life. Now remember, I was also going through a divorce at this same time. God did not cause me to be sick with cancer, but He did manifest His strength and power. In fact, I was a prime candidate to become a mental health patient, but I didn't.

It was during this darkest moment of my life that God made His presence so real. I knew then without a shadow of doubt not only did God care and love me, but He showed it to me a in tangible way. I often reflect on those six weeks, and I am beyond grateful for life and His ways of expressing to me that I did matter to Him. His timing to demonstrate this tangible expression manifested during the time I needed it the most. I could have easily taken the negative report I received, the lack of support from family and friends, and the divorce as an opportunity to have a pity party, but I did not. I chose to find the good in all of it.

Forgiving ourselves gives us the liberty to find the good in everything. Not only does it help us to find the good in everything, it also lessens the blows we receive in life. The moment I decided to forgive myself, there was a release of pain. The more I submitted to the process of forgiving myself, I noticed the pain I was harboring dissipating. Choosing not to forgive yourself is damaging to you first and then to those who are closest to you.

When there is no forgiveness of self, it's like lighting a match and holding it to your bosom. Eventually, the fire you hold close in your bosom will begin to spread to other areas of your body. This kind of pain cannot be contained. Refusing to forgive yourself will spread like wildfire, often manifesting through sickness and disease.

You and I deserve to walk in freedom. We deserve the ability to love others freely. Now that we have taken ownership for our contributions, it makes logical sense to address the opposite spectrum—examining those things we thought were right. It took me a long time to realize the importance of releasing the wrongs I thought were right. As you and I walk through this journey together, I encourage you to do the same. You can release unhealthy ways of doing things that you witnessed and deemed healthy. When we are exposed to healthy relationships and the results of positive choices, we have a standard or a pattern.

When there is no reference point, we often establish our own. This principle can be applied to any relationship including business. While you and I may have started out ignorantly, we do not have to remain in that place. We owe it to ourselves to change the trajectory for the remainder of our lives and those that will soon come behind us.

Ignorance is not an excuse to remain the same. Get up from the floor and brush yourself off.

For those who may lack those healthy examples, I implore you to seek out mentors and those who can serve as role models for you. Read books and study successful and happy couples. This will help you understand what's needed to develop the type of relationship desired. I remember vividly observing other couples in public. I would pay attention to how the man [husband] interacted and communicated with his girlfriend or wife, and I would closely watch her response to his actions. It was from those observations the light bulbs went off for me. It was clear to me, that I was accustomed to being in unhealthy relationships. I had to first deal with my open wounds, then transform my thinking and behavior. That was the only way I could embrace the true meaning of covenant and essentially build a family unit of wholeness.

As we embark upon 2021, there should be no excuses. If you are not sure of what being healthy looks like, you can grab your laptop, smartphone, or any other device with the latest technology to help you live your best life. There are a slew of things, quality traits, signs that are available to aid in the development of a healthy foundation. When we know better, we can begin to do better. Again, truth must be the foundation of forgiveness.

The great news is knowing we get the opportunity to start over. As long as there is breath in our bodies, we always have an opportunity to right the wrongs. For those things that cannot be corrected, you can correct the course of the next moment, and the next decision. The moment you decide that you no longer want to hold yourself hostage in your mind is the day you can take the handcuffs off and begin to walk in freedom.

The great news about walking in freedom is starting anew. We get an opportunity to love without the fire of unforgiveness locked in our bosoms. We have an opportunity to learn from our mistakes. Let's agree that yesterday did in fact happen. Let's also agree that yesterday has its place in which it belongs—the past. Let every negative situation remain in the past.

Of course, there are times, in which you may be tempted to rehearse negative words that were once said to you, but take control of those thoughts by verbally saying, "The mistakes I have made, I have forgiven myself, learned from them and have moved forward. There is no place in my life at this moment for me to relive what has already happened. I choose not to take fire unto my bosom."

In doing so, we are acknowledging where we were in the past, yet it has passed. Once we can verbally say that it has passed from us, we are not plagued with the possibilities of picking "it" back up.

A lot of mistakes are often repeated simply because an acknowledgment was never made of where the person used to be. If you do not recognize that place you are bound to revisit it. As you progress to this place, you will discover eventually that some of the expectations you once had came from a place of brokenness. I will give you a prime example. My father was not present in my life. I was not fortunate to have his affirmation before he died in 2014. Prior to his death, I did not realize the expectations that should have been reserved for my father only, were subconsciously placed on the men I dated and eventually married. So, if my ex-husband did something to trigger that empty feeling in me, I would immediately think back to how my father was never present. It all evolved around broken promises. Therefore, if my ex-husband was unable to do something, internally I perceived that he was just like my father and made empty promises.

    I am not saying my ex-husband should be excused for not doing all he could have done; however, I do recognize I was wrong for instantly placing what my father never did onto him. Those were two isolated incidents that should have remained independent from each other. The actions of my ex-husband were not a result of what my father failed to do. It took me a while to realize that the expectations of my father should never be transferred to my then husband or any other man.

    I had to allow my heart to heal from the lies, disappointments, and abandonment from my father. It was only after I completely healed that I was able to receive and truly love another man from a healthy place. Prior to this realization I constantly made the mistake of trying to love from that place of brokenness and hurt.

    There is a two-sided spectrum of forgiveness. No one can make the choice for you to forgive. I had to make the decision that I no longer wanted to hold a fire to my bosom that would soon contaminate everything and everyone I knew or met. My dear friends, you must do the same thing. I have not shared my personal experiences to point the finger or to look down on anyone, but instead, to encourage you so that you can do the same.

The magnitude of the pain is irrelevant, simply because pain does not discriminate. It all hurts the same and can have negative lifelong affects should you choose not to forgive. Forgiving yourself determines the condition of your relationships with others as well as the condition and quality of life you will partake in. In order to live your best life, forgiveness must be present. It is impossible to do so without letting go.

CHAPTER 14

THE BENEFITS OF REJECTION AND ABANDONMENT

Without personally experiencing rejection and abandonment, I would have never discovered hidden truths regarding each one. The saying, "Sticks and stones may break my bones, but words will never hurt me," was a complete lie. Not only do words hurt, but actions also hurt. Let's face it, when it comes to "rejection" there is nothing positive about the word.

I used to believe that no good thing could possibly come from rejection, abandonment and being blacklisted. I remember the day as if it was yesterday…. After receiving the cancer diagnosis, I somehow thought I would have a few friends that would stick around for support. There were a couple of friends that remained, but initially, I became bitter because I felt like they all abandoned me. Equally, I became bitter toward my family because of their absence. As I went through radiation treatments, one of my cousins sacrificed to come to my home and do laundry, prepare multiple meals, and to clean.

During my alone time, God revealed to me that He purposely moved people away so that I could hear Him clearly. God was also preparing me to write the very book you are reading. He literally gave me the words for this book. He did not want my opinion or the opinions of others to interfere with what He had predestined for me.

With lots of free time on my hands, I began to hear what He needed you to read.

Rejection and abandonment are very difficult. They are at the root of a lot of issues in families and relationships. On top of those, I know what it feels like to be blacklisted.

Everyone knows the harmful effect rejection can have on anyone. Instead of focusing on the harmful effects, try finding the good that came as a result of the rejection you have experienced. If you do not find peace in the middle of the rejection, the enemy will cause you to feel defeated, lonely and empty.

Life's pitfalls and valley experiences must be examined through the proper lenses.

I recall being wrongly terminated from my job and feeling various emotions. I had plans of purchasing my first home. As bad as I felt for not being able to reach my goal of becoming a homeowner, that wrongful termination was the best thing that could have happened to me.

I was able to receive unemployment, which was the same as my take home pay. It enabled me to focus on graduate school, by increasing an additional class per semester. I was also able to spend more time with my children and I was able to volunteer at my daughters' schools. Being terminated afforded me the opportunity to do things that I was not able to do while working a full-time job. As I shifted my thinking and view, being terminated was not so bad after all.

As the oldest of two children, I experienced rejection from my mother, father, grandmother, aunts and uncles. The rejection caused me to build walls around myself as a defense mechanism. As I became older and continued to experience rejection from different people, I became an expert at shielding myself from pain. Rejection was protection in disguise. As badly as I wanted to feel included in what I assumed was great, it turned out to be the opposite.

It was not until I became an adult that I realized my father was a frequent drug user. My father's drug of choice was cocaine. The feeling of wanting to be affirmed and held by him overshadowed this truth. Only God knew the impact drugs would have had on me, and for that reason alone, I am convinced I was protected through my father's rejection. Yes, he should have been a better father to me, but not at the expense of me being exposed to drugs or worse.

Not only was I protected from my father through rejection, but I was also protected through rejection from the men that I thought I wanted to date. Men who rejected me, were protection in disguise. If we are not careful, we can become bitter because of rejection. The very thing in which we have convinced ourselves that we need is often what holds the key to our spiritual, physical, mental, and emotional contamination.

From the many encounters of rejection, my built-in defense mechanism became my refuge. I discovered that instead of shielding myself from pain, I needed to draw closer to God. The more I experienced rejection from my family, the more I rehearsed who I was to God.

I repeated, "I am the apple of His eye and He is concerned about me and those things that I am concerned about." As I spoke positive affirmations, the negative words were eventually silenced. With fewer thoughts on how someone viewed me negatively, it also encouraged me to discover personal interests and pursue my goals.

Once I took my focus off everything that was not conducive for me, and I gave myself permission to accomplish multiple major goals. I earned my graduate degree, and took my dream vacations to Hawaii, Niagara Falls and Canada. I started my own businesses and nonprofit organizations. It is proven that when an individual becomes consumed by the opinions of others, it hinders their ability to move forward.

The freedom that comes with the liberty of being the best version of yourself can only come as a result of being comfortable in your own skin. Being rejected helped me to be ok with being alone. I am not declaring you must be alone; however, what I am saying is it is beneficial to function away from a crowd.

We must master the art of loving ourselves before we can offer the best of ourselves to others. If I don't enjoy my own company, then how can I expect someone else to want to spend time with me? As bad as rejection can be, there are quite a few good things that stem from being rejected. No matter how bad of an experience you or I may have encountered, we must be mindful in knowing there is always some good to come from it.

If we choose to see things differently, we have the power to shift any negative situation and turn it around for our good. If truth be told, the bad will always be among us. Let's face it, if you had not gone through everything you have endured and overcome, can you honestly say you would still be the man or woman you are today? I can help answer that question for you, NO! The rejection caused you to dig deep within to discover self-love and self-acceptance. When rejection is handled properly, you are better equipped to dance to the beat of your own drum, even if that means dancing alone.

Dancing alone requires great inner strength and resolve. Instead of building walls, it builds confidence. Dancing alone isn't something that most people set out to do. In fact, we all like companionship, therefore we are pushed into dancing alone through an unfavorable situation. Keep in mind, although rejected, God delivers us from some people to keep us "set apart" for His glory. We've discussed the contamination that can occur if we seek to fit into certain groups or maintain certain relationships. Thus, dancing alone is sometimes very necessary.

I will share the perspectives of four different individuals that experienced rejection and abandonment but also benefited from it. Even a blemished apple can be used. You may not want to eat it, but it still has nutritional value when consumed in a smoothie.

When we limit our use of any hand that may have been dealt to us, we limit ourselves from a plethora of new beginnings. We give the biggest keys to our destiny to the people that rejected us.

When the light came on, we discovered they lacked the capacity to fill the empty cups in our lives. We gave them our cups only for them to be filled with air. There are four perspectives that share similarities of "the cup." The four perspectives include the story of the Samaritan woman at the well, Moses, Paul and Jesus.

We all have heard the story of the woman at the well. Her story is found in the Bible in John chapter 4. The Samaritan woman knew she had an unfavorable reputation and took it upon to herself to go to the well for water during the time of day she would least likely meet other women. Upon meeting Jesus, she knew it was also uncommon for people of her ethnic group to mix and mingle with Jews.

During her time at the well, she met a man who she thought was a regular Joe. But from looking at Him, she knew that He was of Jewish decent, therefore, she assumed He would avoid her based on the racial prejudices of their time. But instead, He asked her for some water. He spoke with authority and compassion and offered her what no man has ever offered, Living Water.

His response to her, ignited something on the inside of her, and she was hungry for the Living Water that He offered. It was different from what she was accustomed to. In fact, He offered her the water because He knew what she was looking for could not be found in the same cups she'd previously received. It was her rejection and reputation that caused her to be found by Him. If she had visited the well during normal times, she would have missed the divine opportunity with Jesus.

As she left the well, she began to tell men about her encounter with Jesus. It was her rejection that qualified her to instantly become a disciple of Jesus. She excitedly shared the things Jesus told her. Her testimony caused the men listening to her to also want to know Jesus. No one else was able to get the attention of the men, but it was the rejection of the Samaritan woman that led to their coming to know Jesus.

> *"Jesus saith unto her, "Woman, believe me, the hour cometh, when ye shall neither in this mountain, nor yet at Jerusalem, worship the Father. Ye worship ye know not what: we know what we worship: for salvation is of the Jews. But the hour cometh, and now is, when the true worshippers shall worship the Father in spirit and in truth: for the Father seeketh such to worship him. God is a spirit: and they that worship him must worship Him in spirit and in truth. The woman saith unto Him, I know that Messias cometh, which is called Christ: when He is come, He will tell us all things. Jesus saith unto her, I that speak unto thee am He. And upon this came His disciples, and marveled that He talked with the woman: yet no man said, What sleekest thou? or, Why talkest thou with her? The woman then left her waterpot, and went her way into the city, and saith to the men, Come, see a man, which told me all things that ever I did: is not this the Christ? Then they went out of the city, and came unto Him"* (John 4:21-30).

The Samaritan woman experienced rejection from other women, however, it did not prohibit her from boldly sharing her encounter with Jesus. Somehow, we misinterpret rejection to mean that there is something wrong with us. In reality, rejection serves a twofold purpose: It protects us from the toxicity that may try to invade our lives, and it also pushes us deeper into the arms of our Savior. The Living water that flowed through her veins became deliverance for others. Therefore, rejection is necessary to move us into a greater purpose. We must rise beyond our current situations and circumstances to pass the baton of hope and deliverance to future generations.

Somehow, we misinterpret rejection to mean that there is something wrong with us. In reality, rejection serves a twofold purpose: It protects us from the toxicity that may try to invade our lives, and it also pushes us deeper into the arms of our Savior. The Samaritan woman experienced rejection from other women, however, it did not prohibit her from boldly sharing her encounter with Jesus. The Living water that flowed through her veins became deliverance for others. Therefore, rejection is necessary to move us into a greater purpose. We must rise beyond our current situations and circumstances to pass the baton of hope and deliverance to future generations.

Remember, the most effective advertisers are those that believe 100% in what they are selling. It is impossible to give hope if you do not have hope on the inside of your heart. You, me, and the Samaritan woman all have one thing in common, the experience of rejection. We also have the redemptive, unconditional, and sacrificial love of Christ.

Ephesians 1 teaches us that we have been adopted into the family of God. That cancels all rejection; we are accepted in the beloved. Thus, rejection can no longer hold us captive with its bitter grip. We have the power to overcome.

The second perspective I will share is that of Moses. The story of Moses is another familiar story that many may have heard. It is found in the Bible in Exodus chapter 1. There was a decree in Egypt to kill every male child. Moses' mother purposely abandoned her son with the hopes of saving his life. She safely placed him in a basket and placed the basket in the river. As the basket began to flow in the river, she managed to keep her eye on the basket from dry land. She placed the basket in the river in hopes that the basket would be discovered by the king's daughter.

Her plan worked. The daughter of Pharaoh found the basket and hired Moses' mother to nurse him. If Moses' mother did not move swiftly, Moses could have been killed along with the other male children. The fact is that Moses' abandonment worked for him. Moses' story of divine intervention should encourage every individual who has experienced abandonment.

The very thing they hated could have been the very thing that saved their lives. Only his mother did not hate him, her abandonment was done out of love. It is hard to fathom someone abandoning a baby out of love. Love would cause you to sacrifice your own life for your child. There are many who place children up for adoption for their emotional and physical well-being. They knew that they simply could not give the child(ren) what they needed at the time. Moses mother knew that her baby's salvation, depended upon her willingness to believe God would spare his life.

I can only imagine how his mother felt as she placed him in the basket in the Nile River. The hope in her heart for a better life for Moses outweighed all negative possibilities. Yes, he could have been eaten by alligators. Yes, water could have filled the basket causing him to drown. Yes, the basket could have taken one wrong turn. Nevertheless, hope caused her to send him beyond her fears.

"And when she could no longer hide him, she took for him an ark of bulrushes, and daubed it with slime and with pitch, and put the child therein; and she laid it in the flags by the river's brink. And his sister stood afar off, to wit what would be done to him. And the daughter of Pharaoh came down to wash herself at the river; and her maidens walked along by the river's side; and when she saw the ark among the flags, she sent her maid to fetch it. And when she had opened it, she saw the child: and, behold, the babe wept. And she had compassion on him and said. This is one of the Hebrews' children. Then said his sister to Pharaoh's daughter, Shall I go and call to thee a nurse of the Hebrew women, that she may nurse the child for thee? And Pharaoh's daughter said to her, Go. And the maid went and called the child's mother. And Pharaoh's daughter said unto her, Take this child away and nurse it for me, and I will give thee thy wages. And the woman took the child and nursed it. And the child grew, and she brought him unto Pharaoh's daughter, and he became her son. And she called his name Moses: and she said, Because I drew him out of the water" (Exodus 2:3-10).

We learn from Moses' story of abandonment that there is good to be found in the most difficult situations. It was not until I became an adult and understood why I was abandoned by my earthly father. I am convinced my life would have turned out differently if he never abandoned me. I am 99.98% positive that I would have been exposed to his lifestyle as a drug user and could have potentially followed a very similar path. The more I thought about all I was protected from, the more I became grateful for his selfish decision to not be a constant part of my life.

I do believe the pain I experienced as a result of him not being present may have been minor compared to the possibility of becoming addicted to drugs. A few years prior to my father passing away, I asked him if he was currently using drugs and he confirmed that he was. Instantly, I knew my life would have taken a different route if he were an active part of my life. At that moment, I understood the protection of God. It became easier to forgive him for not being there and the weight of bitterness was easy to release.

At the time of his death, I was sad to see him die, but overjoyed that I'd forgiven him before he became sick. I think about him and I miss him, but I also enjoy the peace I have regarding my actions. The moment I decided to forgive him, I realized that my decision was not predicated on what he was going to do. I forgave him because I was ready to release all of the negative feelings.

Before his death, I was able to serve him with love. I was free from bitterness and free from anger. I do wish he was alive to witness me graduate with my Associates degree as a sign language interpreter. Growing up with deaf parents wasn't easy, but I wanted to give back to them by learning American Sign Language. I do wish he'd chosen a different route and made better decisions, but I had to resolve the matter in my mind and heart that things happened the way they were supposed to happen. Otherwise, I would have lived a life of constant mental torment consumed with the what-ifs? What-ifs never seem to run out. They are like the Energizer Bunny; they keep going and going and going. In both examples above, both the woman at the well and Moses, we can see that rejection and abandonment, can work out for our highest good. In both cases, there is a twist of Divine protection.

The third perspective is taken from the story of Saul being transformed to Paul. Saul was notorious in bringing harm to Christians, until he had an experience himself. The story of Saul's transformation is found in the Bible in the book of Acts chapter 9. Paul's conversion shed light on the lack of faith of new converts. Saul's transformation was not easy to receive, because he persecuted Christians so fervently. Therefore, it was difficult for most Christians during that era to believe.

Because of the murder and torture of Christians, it was probably hard for them to trust that the person who stood so adamantly against them, was now a part of them. In fact, the Apostle Paul describes the manner in which he persecuted Christians in Galatians 1:13, "For you have heard of my former conduct in Judaism, how I persecuted the church of God beyond measure and tried to destroy it."

On one hand, I can understand why the new converts would be upset at Paul. However, on the other hand, it would reveal the power of God to truly transform. The focus has always been on Paul and his heinous acts against Christians, but no one talks about the lack of faith that existed in the new church. The church teaches the power of transformation, and Jesus, but dismissed it all when Paul was transformed. The rejection that Paul experienced was from those who were of the same faith. It is easier to accept persecution from those that do not live out righteousness. It is a different matter, when the persecution comes from the house of God.

> *'But the Lord said unto him, "Go thy way: for he is a chosen vessel unto me, to bear my name before the Gentiles, and kings, and the children of Israel: for I will shew him how great things he must suffer for my name's sake. And Ananias went his way, and entered into the house; and putting his hands on him said, Brother Saul, the Lord, even Jesus, that appeared unto thee in the way as thou camest, hath sent me, that thou mightiest receive thy sight, and be filled with the Holy Ghost. And immediately there fell from his eyes as it had been scales: and he received sight forthwith, and rose, and was baptized. And when he had received meat, he was strengthened. Then was Saul certain days with the disciples which were at Damascus. And straightway he preached Christ in the synagogues, that he is the Son of God. But all that heard him were amazed, and said; Is not this he that destroyed them which called on this name in Jerusalem, and came hither for that*

intent, that he might bring them bound unto the chief priests? But Saul increased the more in strength, and confounded the Jews which dwelt at Damascus, proving that this very Christ. And after that many days were fulfilled; the Jews took counsel to kill him" (Acts 9:15-23).

Paul's rejection from the new church caused him to continue to reach people who were intended to be excluded from the plan of salvation. Paul's voice was needed. God used Paul to write over half of the New Testament from Jail. He was often isolated and abandoned. In 2 Timothy 4:9, Paul urges Timothy to visit him as soon as he could because Demas, who stood with him during his first imprisonment deserted him in Rome because he feared for his own life.

Paul was required to endure rejection for the common good of the people. If you and I are honest, we can identify some things in our lives that have caused us to experience pain so that someone else may benefit from it. Everything that we go through is not about us. There are times in life where we may have to take one for the team.

"Taking one for the team" will force an individual to put their desires and needs on the back burner for the sake of someone else. "Taking one for the team" is equivalent to having a thorn in the flesh. The purpose of the thorn is to keep an individual in a state of humility. Paul was grateful for the opportunity to serve, especially on the team of people he was known for persecuting.

It was my intent to uncover the pattern that is repeated in each of the Biblical narratives. Rejection and abandonment can be viewed as a positive instead of a negative. We see that something positive resulted from what was perceived as bad.

Allow me to clarify, I am not saying hardships are good for people, but I am saying life could have been worse than the experience of the individual. Shifting our perspective will always cause us to see things through a different lens.

The final perspective we will examine is the ministry of Jesus. Jesus went throughout the land performing miracles, signs, and wonders, and His disciples chose to follow Him. Imagine if your friend chose to hang out with you. You didn't ask them, but he or she volunteered to do so. Everything is fine. Everyone is bonding in the group when suddenly, the ringleader is arrested for drug charges. Questions are not asked. Assumptions are made. The group eventually dissolves. Visits are not made to the ringleader, and he or she waits for their court date to present their truth.

Well, this is exactly what happened to Jesus. His disciples abandoned and rejected Him when confronted by the Roman soldiers. His rejection and experience of abandonment would soon be the gateway to His redemptive work on the cross. As Jesus took on rejection and abandonment, he began to usher the will of His Father. If Jesus had refused rejection and abandonment by those he thought loved Him and walked closely with Him in ministry, it is possible we would not know life the way we know it today. His rejection and experience of being abandoned thrust Him into destiny. All of mankind has benefited from His pain.

> *"And immediately, while he yet spake, cometh Judas, one of the twelve, and with him a great multitude with swords and staves, from the chief priests and the scribes and the elders. And he that betrayed him had given them a token, saying, Whomsoever, I shall kiss, that same is he; take him, and lead him away safely. And as soon as he was come, he goeth straightway to him, and saith, Master, master; and kissed him. And they laid their hands on him and took him. And one of them that stood by drew a sword, and smote a servant of the high priest, and cut off his ear. And Jesus answered and said unto them, Are ye come out, as against a thief, with swords and with staves to take me? I was daily with you in the temple teaching and ye took me not: but the scriptures must be fulfilled. And they all forsook him and fled"* (Mark 14:43-50).

Unfortunately, no one is afforded the opportunity to select who will reject or abandon them. It has been proven if we endure the pain of rejection and abandonment, we will discover the waves will usually carry us to a good place. I have seen this to be true in my life and we have seen this to be true in the lives of Moses, Paul, and Jesus, all of whom had a tremendous impact on mankind. If you look, you will find friends, family members, coworkers and neighbors who have experienced their fair share of rejection and abandonment. They bounced back from those waves and are doing good. You, my friend, are capable of riding over waves. You have no idea of all the possibilities the waves of rejection and abandonment will carry you to. You must keep going to the other side of the waves. Surf's up!

CONCLUSION

SURVIVOR ONCE SURVIVOR FOR LIFE

I pray this book has been a blessing to your life. It is important to recognize the survivor within each of us. Each of us has a different story of survival. You must risk disappointing others and share your story. As I mentioned throughout this book, Once a Survivor; Always a Survivor. That means that you have the power within you to overcome every obstacle the enemy will try to place in your path.

As I retraced my steps, I've seen the growth that has taken place. Growth is vital to any level of success. As we grow, we take better care of our mental and emotional well-being. We learn to guard our peace and survive with the discipline to create abundant living. We never want to survive, just to haphazardly say that we are still here. The purpose of our survival must supersede our own goals. It must encompass something that will change the world for the better.

Take confidence in knowing you will look back on the challenges you face today and find the good that came from it. Not everything we go through is detrimental to us. Most of what we go through helps to develop character, integrity and tenacity. From this day forward, do not wallow in where you think you should be. Embrace where you are, knowing you are coming forth at precisely the right time. After all, you have survived some things that should have caused you to lose your mind. You have scars, but you made it through. You had to encourage yourself, but you still made it through. You may have even cried yourself to sleep every night; God has collected each tear you have shed. Your tears are precious to God. Now is not the time to remain in the corner. Come out of that corner fighting with everything within you. Fight as though your life depended on it. Fight as though your inheritance depended on it. Fight with the smell and taste of victory in your mouth.

If you do not know what victory smells or tastes like, then create your own image of what victory looks like. Victory is victory, no matter how you slice it. Whatever it is you have survived, own it. Do not allow anyone to downplay all the hell you have encountered and overcame. You cannot take ownership of other people's insecurities. Some people do not have the courage to go through what you have gone through. Our tests do not look the same, but are prepared for each individual.

Whatever it is that you have gone through that appeared to have taken from you…fight back! Fight back by using your voice, your voice of hope, a voice of healing, and a voice of restoration. God did not allow you to go through all the hell you have been through to be quiet. Consider the assignment God has chosen for you to complete here in the earth. People may be uncomfortable with what you have to say. Say it anyway. Someone is waiting for you to be bold. Take a step of boldness and begin with one word at a time. YOU ARE A SURVIVOR!

ABOUT THE AUTHOR

Sarah S. Johnson is a native of Dallas, Texas. She is mom and role model to her "Just 5" children. A graduate of Southwestern Assemblies of God University with a MA in Biblical and Theological studies, Sarah is forever grateful for EVERY opportunity to serve as a model for God's goodness, grace, mercy, love, strength and healing.

A small token of her gratitude for the platform He has given her through every trial, tear, and disappointment is to reach out with both hands to encourage and help others know that they too can overcome the giants they face. Sarah proves she is a survivor and an overcomer, having endured cancer, divorce, and death of her father within 5 months, she is living proof that God does make good on His promises.

Her relaxing moments consist of cooking and reading a book. She enjoys serving the homeless population through volunteerism with her children. She currently lives in North Carolina.

www.ingramcontent.com/pod-product-compliance
Lightning Source LLC
Chambersburg PA
CBHW070429010526
44118CB00014B/1969